DATA M[ ]L
SCORECARD

Applying the

Industry Standard on

Data Model Quality

first edition

Steve Hoberman

Published by:

2 Lindsley Road
Basking Ridge, NJ 07920 USA

https://www.TechnicsPub.com

Cover design by Mark Brye
Technical reviews by Clifford Heath and R. Raymond McGirt
Edited by Erin Elizabeth Long

All of the data models that appear in this book were created using the Embarcadero® ER/Studio Data Architect® tool, for more information on ER/Studio visit http://www.embarcadero.com/data-modeling.

Embarcadero®, the Embarcadero Technologies logos, and all other Embarcadero Technologies product or service names are trademarks or registered trademarks of Embarcadero Technologies, Inc. Data Model Scorecard® is a registered trademark of Steve Hoberman & Associates, LLC. All other trademarks are property of their respective owners and should be treated as such.

Copyright © 2015 by Technics Publications, LLC

ISBN, print ed.	9781634620826
ISBN, Kindle ed.	9781634620833
ISBN, ePub ed.	9781634620840
ISBN, PDF ed.	9781634620857

First Printing 2015
Library of Congress Control Number: 2015910688

To Jenn.

Contents at a Glance

Table of Contents

Data modeling is the process of discovering, analyzing, and scoping data requirements and then representing these data requirements in a visual format called the "data model." A data model is a set of symbols and text used for communicating a precise representation of an information landscape. As with a model of any landscape, such as a map that models a geographic landscape, certain content is included and certain content excluded to facilitate understanding.

"Discovering" involves determining what information the business needs in its business processes and/or applications such as learning that **Customer** and **Account** are important concepts. "Analyzing" involves clarifying requirements such as coming up with clear definitions for **Customer** and **Account** and understanding the relationship between customers and their accounts. "Scoping" involves working with the business to determine what is most important for a particular project phase such as whether we need both **Savings** and **Checking Accounts** or just **Checking Accounts** for Phase 1. "Representing" means displaying what the information landscape looks like using an unambiguous precise language such as in the following data model:

- Each **Customer** may own one or many **Accounts**.
- Each **Account** must be owned by one or many **Customers**.

Once we document these requirements on the data model, we can then communicate them to business and information technology (IT) players involved in application development such as business users, business analysts, data modelers, data architects, database administrators, developers, testers, and managers.

Data models are the main medium used to communicate data requirements from business to IT, and within IT from analysts, modelers, and architects to database designers and developers. Regardless of whether the underlying database technology is a Relational Database Management System (RDBMS) such as Oracle or Teradata, or a NoSQL database such as MongoDB or Hadoop, we still need a way to communicate data requirements. Therefore, we need data models!

Our data models need to be of high quality to support current requirements yet also gracefully accommodate future requirements. The Data Model Scorecard® is a tool you can use to improve the quality of your organization's data models.

Many of my consulting assignments are dedicated to applying the Data Model Scorecard to my client's data models and making recommendations to improve the design. This book will show you how to apply the Data Model Scorecard. This book is written for people who build, use, or review data models. There are three sections.

In Section I, *Data Modeling and the Need for Validation*, you will receive a short data modeling primer in Chapter 1, understand why it is important to get the data model right in Chapter 2, and learn about the Data Model Scorecard in Chapter 3.

In Section II, *Data Model Scorecard Categories*, we will explore each of the ten categories of the Data Model Scorecard. There are ten chapters in this section, each chapter dedicated to a specific Scorecard category:

- Chapter 4: Correctness
- Chapter 5: Completeness
- Chapter 6: Scheme
- Chapter 7: Structure
- Chapter 8: Abstraction
- Chapter 9: Standards
- Chapter 10: Readability
- Chapter 11: Definitions
- Chapter 12: Consistency
- Chapter 13: Data

Each of these chapters ends with a summary of that category's checks.

In Section III, *Validating Data Models*, we will prepare for the model review (Chapter 14), cover pointers during the model review (Chapter 15), and then review a data model based upon an actual project (Chapter 16).

All of the data models that appear in this book were created using the Embarcadero® ER/Studio Data Architect® tool. For more information on ER/Studio, visit http://www.embarcadero.com/data-modeling. You can download a free trial of the tool at http://www.embarcadero.com/downloads.

Section I
Data Modeling and the Need for Validation

In this section you will receive a short data modeling primer in Chapter 1, understand the reasons it is important to get the data model right in Chapter 2, and learn about the Data Model Scorecard in Chapter 3.

Chapter 1
Data Modeling Primer

This chapter will provide a brief overview of data model components including how to read a data model. For more content, please refer to my book *Data Modeling Made Simple*.

ENTITIES

An entity represents a collection of information about something that the business deems important and worthy of capture. Each entity is identified by a noun or noun phrase, and it fits into one of six categories: who, what, when, where, why, or how. Here is a definition of each of these entity categories along with examples:

Category	Definition	Examples
Who	Person or organization of interest to the enterprise. That is, "*Who* is important to the business?" Often a *Who* is associated with a role such as Customer or Vendor.	Employee, Patient, Player, Suspect, Customer, Vendor, Student, Passenger, Competitor, Author
What	Product or service of interest to the enterprise. It often refers to what the organization makes that keeps it in business. That is, "*What* is important to the business?"	Product, Service, Raw Material, Finished Good, Course, Song, Photograph, Title
When	Calendar or time interval of interest to the enterprise. That is, "*When* is the business in operation?"	Time, Date, Month, Quarter, Year, Semester, Fiscal Period, Minute
Where	Location of interest to the enterprise. Location can refer to actual places as well as electronic places. That is, "*Where* is business conducted?"	Mailing Address, Distribution Point, Website URL, IP Address
Why	Event or transaction of interest to the enterprise. These events keep the business afloat. That is, "*Why* is the business in business?"	Order, Return, Complaint, Withdrawal, Deposit, Compliment, Inquiry, Trade, Claim
How	Documentation of the event of interest to the enterprise. Documents record the events such as a Purchase Order recording an Order event. That is, "*How* does the business keep track of events?"	Invoice, Contract, Agreement, Purchase Order, Speeding Ticket, Packing Slip, Trade Confirmation

Entity instances are the occurrences or values of a particular entity. Think of a spreadsheet as being an entity where the column headings represent the pieces of information that may be recorded for each entity. Each spreadsheet row containing the actual values represents an entity instance. The entity **Customer** may have multiple customer instances with the names Bob, Joe, Jane, and so forth. The entity **Account** can have instances of Bob's checking account, Bob's savings account, Joe's brokerage account, and so on.

Entities may be described at conceptual, logical, and physical levels of detail. The conceptual means the high level business solution to a business process or application effort frequently defining scope and important terminology, the logical means the detailed business solution to a business process or application effort, and the physical means the detailed technical solution to an application effort.

For an entity to be relevant at a conceptual level, it must be both basic and critical to the business. What is basic and critical depends very much on the scope. At a universal level, there are certain concepts common to most companies such as **Customer**, **Product**, and **Employee**. Making the scope slightly narrower, a given industry may have certain unique concepts. **Campaign**, for example, will be a valid concept for the advertising industry but perhaps not for all other industries. In the publishing industry, **Author**, **Title**, and **Order** are conceptual entities, shown as names within rectangles:

Author	**Title**	**Order**

Entities described at a logical level represent the business in more detail than at the conceptual level. Frequently, a conceptual entity represents many logical data model entities. Logical entities contain properties, often called "attributes," which we will discuss in the next section. Here are three logical entities based upon the previous conceptual entities:

Author

Author Tax Identifier
Author Birth Date
Author Last Name
Author First Name

Title

Title ISBN
Title Name
Subtitle Name
Retail Price Amount

Order

Order Number
Order Placement Date
Order Scheduled Delivery Date

At a physical level, the entities correspond to technology-specific objects such as database tables in a relational database management system (RDBMS) or collections in the NoSQL database MongoDB. The physical level is similar to the logical level but may include compromises that were needed to make up for deficiencies in technology, often related to performance or storage.

Below are physical entities based upon the previous logical entities. The physical entities also contain database-specific information such as the format and length of an attribute (**Author Last Name** is 50 characters) and whether the attribute is required to have a value (**Author Tax Identifier** is not null and therefore required to have a value, but **Author Birth Date** is null and therefore not required to have a value).

Author

Author Tax Identifier (PK)	CHAR(9)	NOT NULL
Author Birth Date	DATETIME	NULL
Author Last Name	CHAR(50)	NULL
Author First Name	CHAR(30)	NULL

Title

Title ISBN (PK)	CHAR(13)	NOT NULL
Title Name	CHAR(100)	NULL
Subtitle Name	CHAR(100)	NULL
Retail Price Amount	DECIMAL(5,2)	NULL

Order

Order Number (PK)	CHAR(5)	NOT NULL
Order Placement Date	DATE	NULL
Order Scheduled Delivery Date	DATE	NULL

In an RDBMS, these physical entities become database tables or views. In NoSQL databases, these physical entities become transformed depending on the underlying technology. For example, in MongoDB, a document-based database, these entities become collections. The general term "structure" will be used to refer to the underlying database components independent of whether the database is a RDBMS or NoSQL solution.

ATTRIBUTES

An attribute is an individual piece of information whose values identify, describe, or measure instances of an entity. The attribute **Claim Number** identifies each claim. The attribute **Student Last Name** describes the student. The attribute **Gross Sales Amount** measures the monetary value of a transaction.

As with entities, attributes can be described at conceptual, logical, and physical levels. An attribute at the conceptual level must be a concept both basic and critical to the business. We do not usually think of attributes as concepts, but depending on the business need, they can be. When I worked for a telecommunications company, **Phone Number** was an attribute that was so important to the business that it was represented on a number of conceptual data models.

An attribute on a logical data model represents a business property. Each attribute shown contributes to the business solution and is independent of any technology including software and hardware. For example, **Author Last Name** is an attribute because it has business significance regardless of whether records are kept in a paper file or within the fastest database out there. An attribute on a physical data model represents a database column. The attribute **Author Last Name** might be represented as the column **AUTH_LAST_NM** within the RDBMS table **AUTH** or represented as the field name **AuthorLastName** within the MongoDB collection **LibraryCardCatalog**.

DOMAINS

The complete set of all possible values that an attribute can be assigned is called a domain. A domain involves a set of validation criteria that can be applied to more than one attribute. For example, the domain **Date**, which contains all possible valid dates, can be assigned to any of these attributes:

- **Employee Hire Date**
- **Order Entry Date**
- **Claim Submit Date**
- **Course Start Date**

An attribute must never contain values outside of its assigned domain. The domain values are defined by specifying the actual list of values or a set of rules. **Employee Gender Code**, for example, may be limited to the domain of `female` and `male`. **Employee Hire Date** may initially be assigned the rule that its domain contain only valid dates, for example. Therefore, this may include values such as:

- February 15th, 2005
- 25 January 1910
- 20150410
- March 10th, 2050

Because **Employee Hire Date** is limited to valid dates, it does not include February 30th, for example. An attribute may restrict a domain with additional rules. For example, by restricting the **Employee Hire Date** domain to dates earlier than today's date, we would eliminate March 10th, 2050. By restricting **Employee Hire Date** to YYYYMMDD (that is, year, month, and day concatenated), we would eliminate all the examples given except for 20150410. Another way of refining this set of values is to restrict the domain of **Employee Hire Date** to dates that fall on a Monday, Tuesday, Wednesday, Thursday, or Friday (that is, the typical workweek).

There are three basic domain types:

- **Format domains** specify the standard types of data one can have in a database. For example, Integer, Character(30), and Date are all format domains.
- **List domains** are similar to a drop-down list. They contain a finite set of values from which to choose. List domains are refinements of format domains. The format domain for **Order Status Code** might be Character(10). This domain can be further defined through a list domain of possible values {Open, Shipped, Closed, Returned}.
- **Range domains** allow all values that are between a minimum and maximum value. For example, **Order Delivery Date** must be between today's date and three months in the future. As with list domains, range domains are a refined version of a format domain.

RELATIONSHIPS

A relationship between entities indicates that the instances of those entities may be related in some meaningful way. Each relationship may define rules around when and how many instances are related. Relationships are depicted as a line between the two entities. However, some kinds of modeling allow more than two, and these have different depictions. If the two entities are

Employee and **Department**, the relationship can capture the rules "Each **Employee** must work for one **Department**" and "Each **Department** may contain one or many **Employees**."

In a relationship between two entities, cardinality captures how many instances from one entity participate in the relationship with instances of the other entity. It is represented by the symbols that appear on each end of a relationship line. Cardinality specifies one kind of data rule that can be enforced. Without cardinality, the most we can say about a relationship is that two entities are connected in some way through a rule. For example, **Employee** and **Department** have some kind of relationship, but we may not know more than this. Note that the same two entities may be related in more than one way; for example each **Department** may contain one or many **Employees**, but there could be a separate relationship capturing the **Employee** who manages that **Department**.

For cardinality, we can choose any combination of zero, one, or many. *Many* (some people read it as *more*) means any number greater than zero. Specifying zero or one allows us to capture whether or not an entity instance is *required* in a relationship. Specifying one or many allows us to capture *how many* of a particular instance participates in a given relationship.

Because our diagramming approach has only three cardinality symbols, we can't specify an exact number[1] (other than through documentation), as in "A **Car** contains four **Tires**." We can only say, "A **Car** may contain many **Tires**." Each of the cardinality symbols is illustrated here with **Author** and **Title**:

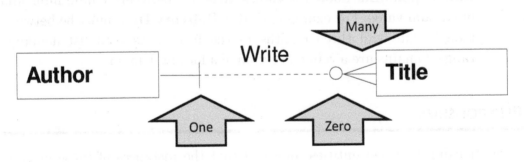

---

[1] Note that if you are using the Class Diagram in the Unified Modeling Language (UML for short), you can specify exact numbers in cardinality.

The business rules in this example are:

- Each **Author** may write one or many **Titles**.
- Each **Title** must be written by one **Author**.

The small vertical line means *one*. (Looks like a 1, doesn't it?) The circle means *zero*. (Looks like a zero too!) The zero implies optionality and does not exclude the value *one*, so in the above example an author can write just one title, too.

The triangle with a line through the middle means *many*. Some people call the *many* symbol a *crow's foot*. Relationship lines are frequently labeled to clarify the relationship and express the rule that the relationship represents. A data model is a communication tool, and if you think of the entities as nouns, the relationship label is a present tense verb. Therefore, we are just reading this sentence:

- Each **Author** may write one or many **Titles**.

Having a zero in the cardinality makes us use optional-sounding words such as *may* or *can* when reading the relationship. Without the zero, we use mandatory-sounding terms such as *must* or *have to*. So instead of being redundant and saying:

- Each **Author** may write *zero*, one, or many **Titles**.

We take out the word *zero* because it is expressed using the word *may*, which implies the zero:

- Each **Author** may write one or many **Titles**.

Every relationship has a parent and a child. The parent entity appears on the *one* side of the relationship, and the child appears on the *many* side of the relationship. In this example, the parent entity is **Author** and the child entity is **Title**. When I read a relationship, I start with the entity on the *one* side of the relationship (the parent entity) first. "Each **Author** may write one or many **Titles**." I then read the relationship from the many side: "Each **Title** must be written by one **Author**."

I also always use the word *each* in reading a relationship, starting with the parent side. The reason for the word *each* is that you want to specify, on average, how many instances of one entity relate to an entity instance from the other entity.

There are two types of relationships, *identifying* and *non-identifying*. An identifying relationship is shown with a solid line and means that the entity on the many side (the child) is always going to be a dependent entity to the entity on the one side (the parent). The dotted line means that the entity on the many side (the child) is not dependent on the entity on the one side (the parent). Here are both types of relationships:

Identifying relationship	Non-identifying relationship
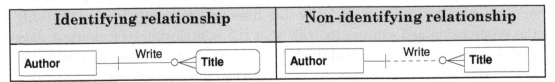	

Independent entities are displayed as rectangles with sharp corners. Dependent entities, such as **Title** under the identifying relationship example, are displayed as rectangles with rounded corners. An independent entity is an entity where each occurrence (instance) can be found using only attributes that it owns. For instance, **Title** under the non-identifying relationship example can be found by an **ISBN** (International Standard Book Number), which is an attribute that belongs to **Title**. A dependent entity such as **Title** under the identifying relationship example can only be found by using at least one attribute from a different entity such as **Author Tax ID** from **Author**.

Let's change the cardinality and now allow a **Title** to be written by more than one **Author**:

This is an example of a many-to-many relationship in contrast to the previous example, which was a one-to-many relationship. The business rules here read as follows:

- Each **Author** may write one or many **Titles**.
- Each **Title** must be written by one or many **Authors**.

Write, in both of our examples, is considered a relationship label. Sometimes the reverse label appears on the relationship line too such as *Written by*. I prefer to show just one relationship label to reduce clutter on the model and also because almost all of the time we can use the same word structure for the reverse label: "Write" and "Written by."

The three levels of granularity (conceptual, logical, and physical) that apply to entities and attributes also apply to the relationships that connect entities. Conceptual relationships are high level rules or navigation paths that connect key concepts. Logical relationships are detailed business rules or navigation paths that enforce the rules between the logical entities. Physical relationships are detailed technology-dependent rules or navigation paths between the physical structures that the relationship connects. These physical relationships may eventually become database constraints in an RDBMS or references in a document-based database such as MongoDB.

KEYS

There is a lot of data out there, but how do you sift through it all to find what you're looking for? That's where keys come in. A key is one or more attributes whose purposes include enforcing rules, efficiently retrieving data, and allowing navigation from one entity to another. This section explains candidate (primary and alternate), surrogate, foreign, and secondary keys.

CANDIDATE KEY (PRIMARY AND ALTERNATE)

A candidate key is one or more attributes that uniquely identify an entity instance. An **ISBN** (International Standard Book Number) is assigned to every title. The **ISBN** uniquely identifies each title and is therefore the title's candidate key. When the **ISBN** for this title, 9781634620826, is entered into many search engines and database systems, the book entity instance Data Model Scorecard will be returned (try it!). **Tax ID** can be a candidate key for an organization in some countries such as the United States. **Account Code** can be a candidate key for an account. A **VIN** (Vehicle Identification Number) identifies a vehicle.

Sometimes a single attribute identifies an entity instance such as **ISBN** for a title. Sometimes it takes more than one attribute to uniquely identify an entity instance. For example, both a **Promotion Type Code** and **Promotion Start**

Date may be necessary to identify a promotion. When more than one attribute makes up a key, we use the term *composite key*. Therefore, **Promotion Type Code** and **Promotion Start Date** together are a composite candidate key for a promotion.

A candidate key has four main characteristics:

- **Unique**. A candidate key value must not identify more than one entity instance (or one real-world thing).
- **Mandatory**. A candidate key may not be empty (also known as *nullable*). Each entity instance must be identified by exactly one candidate key value. Therefore, the number of distinct values of a candidate key is always equal to the number of distinct entity instances. If the entity **Title** has **ISBN** as its candidate key, and if there are 500 title instances, there will also be 500 unique ISBNs.
- **Non-volatile**. A candidate key value on an entity instance should never change.
- **Minimal**. A candidate key should contain only those attributes that are needed to uniquely identify an entity instance. If four attributes are listed as the composite candidate key for an entity, but only three are really needed for uniqueness, then only those three should make up the candidate key.

For example, each **Student** may attend one or many **Classes**, and each **Class** may contain one or many **Students**. Here are some sample instances for each of these entities:

Student

Student Number	First Name	Last Name	Birth Date
SM385932	Steve	Martin	1/25/1958
EM584926	Eddie	Murphy	3/15/1971
HW742615	Henry	Winkler	2/14/1984
MM481526	Mickey	Mouse	5/10/1982
DD857111	Donald	Duck	5/10/1982
MM573483	Minnie	Mouse	4/1/1986
LR731511	Lone	Ranger	10/21/1949
EM876253	Eddie	Murphy	7/1/1992

Attendance

Attendance Date
5/10/2015
6/10/2015
7/10/2015

Class

Class Full Name	Class Short Name	Class Description Text
Data Modeling Fundamentals	Data Modeling 101	An introductory class covering basic data modeling concepts and principles.
Advanced Data Modeling	Data Modeling 301	A fast-paced class covering techniques such as advanced normalization and ragged hierarchies.
Tennis Basics	Tennis One	For those new to the game of tennis; learn the key aspects of the game.
Juggling		Learn how to keep three balls in the air at once!

Based on our definition of a candidate key (and a candidate key's characteristics of being unique, stable, and minimal) what would you choose as the candidate keys for each of these entities?

For **Student**, **Student Number** appears to be a valid candidate key. There are eight students and eight distinct values for **Student Number**. So unlike **Student First Name** and **Student Last Name**, which can contain duplicates like Eddie Murphy, **Student Number** appears to be unique. **Student Birth Date** can also contain duplicates such as 5/10/1982, which is the **Student Birth Date** for both Mickey Mouse and Donald Duck. The combination of **Student First Name**, **Student Last Name**, and **Student Birth Date** may appear to be a valid composite candidate key, but be aware that such a key is not recommended as it might cause problems in some systems.

For **Attendance**, we are currently missing a candidate key. Although the **Attendance Date** is unique in this sample data, we will probably need to know which student attended which class on this particular date, so this definition of **Attendance** is inadequate.

For **Class**, on first glance it appears that any of its attributes are unique and would therefore qualify as a candidate key. However, `Juggling` does not have a **Class Short Name**. Therefore, because **Class Short Name** can be empty, we cannot consider it a candidate key. In addition, one of the characteristics of a candidate key is that it is non-volatile. I know, based on my teaching experience, that class descriptions can change. Therefore, **Class Description Text** also needs to be ruled out as a candidate key, leaving **Class Full Name** as the best option for a candidate key.

Even though an entity may contain more than one candidate key, we can only select one candidate key to be the primary key for an entity. A primary key is the candidate key that has been chosen to be *the preferred* unique identifier for an entity. An alternate key is a candidate key that, although it has the properties of being unique, stable, and minimal, was not chosen as the primary key though it may still be used to find specific entity instances.

We have only one candidate key in the **Class** entity, so **Class Full Name** becomes our primary key. We have to make a choice in **Student**, however, because we have two candidate keys. Which **Student** candidate key would you choose as the primary key?

In selecting one candidate key over another as the primary key, consider succinctness and privacy. Succinctness means if there are several candidate keys, choose the one with the fewest attributes or shortest in length. In terms of privacy, it is possible that one or more attributes within a candidate key will contain sensitive data whose viewing should be restricted. We want to avoid having sensitive data in our entity's primary key because the primary key can propagate as a foreign key and therefore spread this sensitive data throughout our database.

Considering succinctness and security in our example, I would choose **Student Number** over the composite **Student First Name**, **Student Last Name**, and **Student Birth Date**. It is more succinct and contains less sensitive data. Here is our data model with primary and alternate keys:

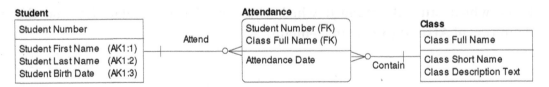

Primary key attributes are shown above the line in the rectangles. You will notice two numbers following the key abbreviation "AK." The first number is the grouping number for an alternate key, and the second number is the ordering of the attribute within the alternate key. So there are three attributes required for the **Student** alternate key: **Student First Name**, **Student Last Name**, and **Student Birth Date**. This is also the order in which the alternate key index will be created because **Student First Name** has a "1" after the colon, **Student Last Name** a "2," and **Student Birth Date** a "3."

Attendance now has as its primary key **Student Number** and **Class Full Name**, which appear to make a valid primary key. Note that the two primary key attributes of **Attendance** are followed by "FK". These are foreign keys, to be discussed shortly.

So to summarize, a candidate key consists of one or more attributes that uniquely identify an entity instance. The candidate key that is determined to be the best way to identify each record in the entity becomes the primary key. The other candidate keys become alternate keys. Keys containing more than one attribute are known as composite keys.

At the physical level, a candidate key is often translated into a unique index.

SURROGATE KEY

A surrogate key is a unique identifier for a table, often a counter, usually fixed-size, and always system-generated without intelligence, so a surrogate key carries no business meaning. (In other words, you can't look at a month identifier of 1 and assume that it represents the **Month** entity instance value of January.) Surrogate keys should not be visible to the business but should remain behind the scenes to allow for more efficient navigation across structures and to facilitate integration across applications.

Surrogate keys are also efficient. You've seen that a primary key may be composed of one or more attributes of the entity. A single surrogate key is more efficient to use than having to specify three or four (or five or six) attributes to locate the single record you're looking for. Surrogate keys are useful for integration, which is an effort to create a single, consistent version of the data. Applications such as data warehouses often house data from more than one application or system. Surrogate keys enable us to record correlations between information about the same entity instance that is identified differently in each source system when those correlations were not obvious from common identifiers.

When using a surrogate key, always make an effort to determine the natural key, which is what the business would consider to be the way to uniquely identify the entity, and then define this natural key as an alternate key. For example, assuming a surrogate key is a more efficient primary key than **Class Full Name**, we can create the surrogate key **Class ID** for **Class** and define an alternate key on the natural key **Class Full Name**, as shown below along with the values in **Class**.

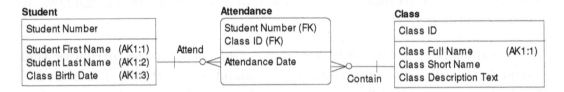

Class ID	Class Full Name	Class Short Name	Class Description Text
1	Data Modeling Fundamentals	Data Modeling 101	An introductory class covering basic data modeling concepts and principles.
2	Advanced Data Modeling	Data Modeling 301	A fast-paced class covering techniques such as advanced normalization and ragged hierarchies.
3	Tennis Basics	Tennis One	For those new to the game of tennis; learn the key aspects of the game.
4	Juggling		Learn how to keep three balls in the air at once!

FOREIGN KEY

The entity on the "one" side of the relationship is called the parent entity, and the entity on the "many" side of the relationship is called the child entity. When we create a relationship from a parent entity to a child entity, the primary key of the parent is copied as a foreign key to the child.

A foreign key is one or more attributes that provide a link to another entity (or in a case of a recursive relationship, where two instances of the same entity may be related, a link to the same entity). At the physical level, a foreign key allows a relational database management system to navigate from one table to another. For example, if we need to know the customer who owns an account, we would want to include the **Customer ID** in the **Account** entity. The **Customer ID** in **Account** is the primary key for **Customer**.

Using this foreign key back to **Customer** enables the database management system to navigate from a particular account or accounts to the customer or customers that own each account. Likewise, the database can navigate from a particular customer or customers to find all of their accounts. Our data modeling tools automatically create a foreign key when a relationship is defined between two entities.

In our **Student/Class** model, there are two foreign keys in **Attendance**. The **Student Number** foreign key points back to a particular student in the **Student** entity, and the **Class ID** foreign key points back to a particular **Class** in the **Class** entity:

Student Number	Class ID	Attendance Date
SM385932	1	5/10/2015
EM584926	1	5/10/2015
EM584926	2	6/10/2015
MM481526	2	6/10/2015
MM573483	2	6/10/2015
LR731511	3	7/10/2015

By looking at these values and recalling the sample values from Table 6.4, we learn that `Steve Martin` and `Eddie Murphy` both attended the `Data Modeling Fundamentals` class on 5/10/2015. `Eddie Murphy` also attended the `Advanced Data Modeling Class` with `Mickey Mouse` and `Minnie Mouse` on 6/10/2015. `Lone Ranger` took `Tennis Basics` (by himself, as usual) on 7/10/2015.

As an aside, note that the current primary key of **Attendance** assumes that a particular student can only attend a particular **Class** once. If the business rule states that a **Student** can attend a **Class** more than once, we would need to modify the primary key of **Attendance** to also include the **Attendance Date**.

SECONDARY KEY

Sometimes there is a need to retrieve data rapidly from a table to answer a business query or meet a certain response time. A secondary key is one or more attributes (if there is more than one attribute, it is called a composite secondary key) that are accessed frequently and need to be retrieved quickly. A secondary key is also known as a non-unique index or inversion entry (IE for short). A secondary key does not have to be unique, stable, nor always contain a value. For example, we can add a secondary key to **Student Last Name** in **Student** to allow for quick retrieval whenever any queries require **Student Last Name**:

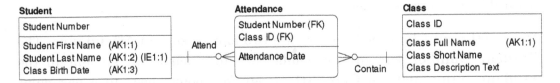

Student Last Name is not unique, as there can be two `Murphys`; it is not stable and can change over time; and although it may be rare, there could be times when we may not know someone's last name, so it can be empty.

SUBTYPES

Subtyping allows grouping the common attributes and relationships of similar or related entities. Subtyping is an excellent way of communicating that certain concepts are very similar and for showing examples. In the publishing industry, an **Author** may write many **PrintVersions** and many **eBooks**:

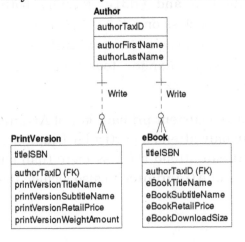

- Each **Author** may write one or many **PrintVersions**.
- Each **PrintVersion** must be written by one **Author**.
- Each **Author** may write one or many **eBooks**.
- Each **eBook** must be written by one **Author**.

Rather than repeat the relationship to **Author**, as well as the common attributes, we can introduce subtyping:

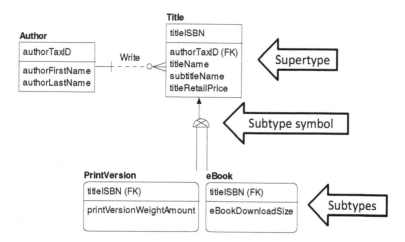

- Each **Author** may write one or many **Titles**.
- Each **Title** must be written by one **Author**.
- Each **Title** may be either a **PrintVersion** or **eBook**.
- Each **PrintVersion** is a **Title**.
- Each **eBook** is a **Title**.

The subtyping relationship implies that all of the relationships and attributes from the supertype also apply to each subtype. Therefore, there is an implied relationship from **Author** to **eBook** as well as from **Author** to **PrintVersion**. Also, the **titleName**, **subtitleName**, and **titleRetailPrice** belong to **PrintVersion** and belong to **eBook**. Note that the primary key of each subtype is a foreign key to the supertype, so it contains the same attributes: in this case, **titleISBN**, which is the identifier for a title.

Not only does subtyping reduce redundancy on a data model, but it makes it easier to communicate similarities across what otherwise would appear to be distinct and separate concepts.

In some cases a supertype can have more than one set of subtypes; for example, a **Person** might be a **Child**, **Teenager**, or **Adult**, and separately from those a **Person** may be **Male** or **Female**.

In some cases the supertype may exist without any of its subtypes but in other cases it cannot; exactly one subtype instance must exist for each supertype. For example, a **Person** may be a **Driver** or may not be; they're still a **Person** in either case. But perhaps a **Bank Account** must always be some particular subtype of account.

Chapter 2
Importance of Data Model Quality

There are three important reasons why we need to get the data model right: Precision, Leverage, and Data Quality. Each of these will be discussed in this chapter.

PRECISION

The data model is a precise representation of an information landscape. *Precision,* with respect to data modeling, means that there is only a single way of reading every symbol and term on the model. If you and I are reading a relationship on a data model, for example, we each read it the exact same way. Precision saves us an incredible amount of effort because we do not have to invest time to come to agreement on what is being represented before discussing it. Because you and I read the relationship the exact same way, we can jump right into discussing whether we agree with it or not instead of starting with what we think it means.

For example, imagine in the publishing industry, someone makes the ambiguous statement, "Books can be ordered". To model this ambiguous statement requires making it precise, which means we need to ask a whole bunch of questions to determine the correct symbols on the relationship line between **Book** and **Order**, as shown on the next page. Once these questions are answered, we build the relationship line with the correct symbols. Now there is only one way to read this relationship:

- Each **Book** may appear on one or many **Orders**.

- Each **Order** may reference one or many **Books**.

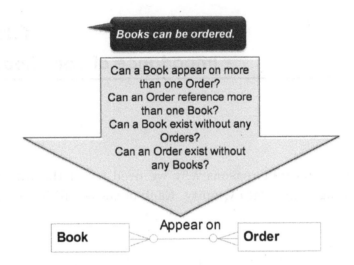

These are some of the many questions that get asked during the data modeling process. Asking and getting answers to questions like these is called *elicitation*, and data modeling includes eliciting and documenting data requirements. There is an iterative process between eliciting and documenting data requirements:

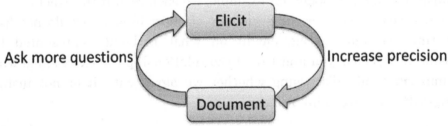

While data modeling, we ask questions to increase the precision of our data model, and then, through the process of documenting our data model, we ask more questions. This loop continues until we are done with our model. A lot of knowledge is gained as the people involved in the modeling process challenge each other about terminology, assumptions, rules, and concepts.

LEVERAGE

Imagine a large boulder that we cannot push. If we have the right kind of stick, we can wedge as much of the stick as possible under the large rock, and with the help of a properly placed fulcrum, push down on the other end of the stick to move the rock. The stick gives us leverage, a magnification of our own power.

The data model is like the stick. Whatever changes are needed to a data model have a magnification effect on the entire application. Leverage is mentioned in Graeme Simsion's and Graham Witt's book *Data Modeling Essentials*: "The key reason for giving special attention to data organization is leverage in the sense that a small change to a data model may have a major impact on the system as a whole."

If a data model was built with subsequent database structures and code on top of it, when the data model required a change it would be magnified as a much larger change to the database structures and code. Adding a new attribute to a logical entity, for example, may take only a minute to complete, but it will take much longer to modify structures and codes and test everything. This is why the data model is like the stick.

For example, imagine we are modeling customer and have included **Customer First Name** and **Customer Last Name** but did not include **Customer Middle Initial**. It would take less than a minute to add this missing attribute, but it could lead to a substantial amount of time to rebuild structures and retest code.

DATA QUALITY

A significant part of the modeling process is defining and representing relationships. Every relationship on a data model is a data quality check. The more relationships we have, the more checks we are performing; therefore, we will have higher data quality in the resulting application. If a **Customer** must have at least one **Account** to be considered a **Customer,** for example, the relationship we define on the data model will enforce that a **Customer** owns at least one **Account**.

We also invest time defining terms on the data model. Clear and concise definitions can help people make better decisions and raise possible issues before development begins. A clear definition for **Account** will increase the chances that only valid account data be loaded into **Account**.

Also, naming standards (Category 6, to be discussed in Chapter 9) help people understand the content of an entity or attribute by its name. For example, following the guidelines of one Prime; zero, one, or more Modifiers; and one Classword help make attributes more easily understood. The attribute name **Account Open Date** is named with enough detail so that it is clear that only the date when the account is opened will be stored in this attribute.

Chapter 3
Data Model Scorecard Overview

Aim, wind, and gravity influence an arrow's trajectory much the same way that deadlines, skills, and experience influence a data model's trajectory, strongly impacting whether a model will reach its target of accuracy, longevity, practicality, and consistency. The archer's score can be quickly calculated, and we can easily see the success or failure of her work. This is where the analogy ends, however, because there is no standard way of measuring the strengths and weaknesses of our models, leaving much up to interpretation, perception, and the test of time. After years of reviewing hundreds of data models, I have formalized a set of data model quality criteria into what I call the Data Model Scorecard®. The Scorecard contains ten clear and distinct criteria for validating a data model. This chapter will summarize the Scorecard.

SCORECARD CHARACTERISTICS

The Data Model Scorecard is a proactive approach to measuring the quality of a data model. The Scorecard has four important characteristics:

- **Highlights not just areas for improvement but also strengths.** The Scorecard not only makes recommendations on areas for improvement, but highlights strengths, giving specific examples of what was done using best design practices. For example, in the same Scorecard report below on the data model for the HAL application, there is a list of both strengths and areas for improvement. Point #25 on this report acknowledges the strength that the model as a perfect balance of abstraction. Abstraction is the use of generic concepts such as "Party" and "Event." Point #125 however captures an area of improvement, namely that when a surrogate key is used, an alternate key should be identified such as on a business key or source system identifier.

> Data Model Scorecard review of HAL application
>
> ...
>
> 25. "There is a perfect balance of abstraction on the model because..."
>
> ...
>
> 125. "A surrogate key requires an alternate key. On this entity you might consider the alternate key to be..."

- **Provides external perspective.** Team rapport remains intact because you, as the reviewer, are not directly criticizing your colleague's data model. Instead, this objective and external scale indicates areas for improvement. The Scorecard uses a points system and several metrics for measuring model quality. Using the Scorecard avoids the emotional situations of having one colleague criticize another colleague's work. Discussions starting off with an emotionally charged phrase such as "I hate what you did there..." usually don't end well. Better to say something like "The Scorecard recommends we make this change to the model..." I have been in extremely fraught data model reviews (even to the point of having someone leave the room crying!), and the Scorecard takes a lot of the emotion out of the equation.

- **Offers straightforward review approach.** The scorecard was designed for even those new to modeling to critique their own models and the models of their colleagues. Follow the approach outlined in this book and you will find yourself providing feedback on data models even if you are not an experienced data modeler! If you are an experienced data modeler, you can use the Scorecard to organize your own thinking in reviewing data models and supplement your thinking with some of the scenarios to look for in Section II.

- **Supports all types of models.** The Scorecard is designed to be used for all model levels of detail: conceptual, logical, and physical. It also supports relational, dimensional, and NoSQL model schemes.

SCORECARD TEMPLATE

Here is the template I complete for each model review:

#	Category	Total score	Model score	%	Comments
1	How well does the model capture the requirements?	15			
2	How complete is the model?	15			
3	How well does the model match its scheme?	10			
4	How structurally sound is the model?	15			
5	How well does the model leverage generic structures?	10			
6	How well does the model follow naming standards?	5			
7	How well has the model been arranged for readability?	5			
8	How good are the definitions?	10			
9	How consistent is the model with the enterprise?	5			
10	How well does the metadata match the data?	10			
	TOTAL SCORE	100			

Each of the ten categories has a total score that relates to the value your organization places on the question. Because we want to express the result as a percentage, the total must equal 100. The model score column contains the results of a particular model review. For example, if a model received 10 on Category 1 ("How well does the model capture the requirements?"), then that is what would go in this column. The % column stores the model score in category divided by the total score in category. For example, receiving 10 out of 15 would lead to 66%. The comments column contains any pertinent information to explain the score in more details or to capture the action items required to fix the model. You may find it useful to always have at least a summary statement in the comments column. Even if there are no issues for a particular category, we can still summarize that the model did well in this category. The last row contains the total score, tallied up for each of the columns to arrive at an overall score for a particular model review.

Here is a summary of each of these ten categories:

1. **How well does the model capture the requirements?** Here we ensure that the data model represents the requirements. If there is a requirement to capture order information, in this category we check the model to make sure it captures order information. If there is a requirement to view **Student Count** by **Semester** and **Major**, in this category we make sure the data model supports this query.

2. **How complete is the model?** Here completeness means two things: completeness of requirements and completeness of metadata. Completeness of requirements means that each requirement that has been requested appears on the model (note we don't check for whether the requirement has been modeled correctly, which is the first category), as well as that the data model only contains what is being asked for and nothing extra. Sometimes we may add structures to the model anticipating they will be used in the near future; we note these sections of the model too during the review because it is always easy to model something and may be hard to deliver (remember "leverage") and may impact the entire project if the modeler includes something that was never asked for. We need to consider the likely cost of including a future requirement in the case that it never eventuates. Completeness of metadata means that all of the descriptive information surrounding the model is present as well; for example, if we are reviewing a physical data model, we would expect formatting and nullability to appear on the data model.

3. **How well does the model match its scheme?** Here we ensure that the model type (conceptual, logical, or physical—and then either relational, dimensional, or NoSQL) of the model being reviewed matches the definition for this type of model. The conceptual defines the scope and captures the business need, the logical is technology-independent and represents a business solution, and the physical is technology-dependent and tuned for performance, security, and development tool constraints, capturing the technical solution. The relational perspective captures business rules, the dimensional perspective captures business questions, and the NoSQL perspective captures how non-RDBMS technologies store data such as in a document or graph.

4. **How structurally sound is the model?** Here we validate the design practices employed to build the model. Assume you were comfortable reading an architectural blueprint and somebody shared their house blueprint with you. If there was a toilet drawn in the middle of the kitchen, a room with no doorway, or a garage drawn in the attic, you would probably catch it. The data model is to a database as a blueprint is to a house. Therefore, you would catch anything structurally incorrect on a data model. For example, a null primary key would be corrected to be required instead of optional.

5. **How well does the model leverage generic structures?** Here we confirm an appropriate use of abstraction. Going from **Customer Location** to a more generic **Location**, for example, allows the design to more easily handle other types of locations such as warehouses and distribution centers. However, it comes with the high price of obscurity and difficulty of enforcing rules. Abstraction must therefore be applied only in situations where it makes the most sense: where flexibility is more important than usability. So we tend to see abstraction more on data warehouse data models over analytical data models, for example.

6. **How well does the model follow naming standards?** Here we ensure correct and consistent naming standards have been applied to the data model. We focus on naming standard structure, term, and style. Structure means that the proper building blocks are being used for entities, relationships, and attributes. For example, a building block for an attribute would be the subject of the attribute such as "Customer" or "Product." Term means that the proper name is given to the attribute or entity. Term also includes proper spelling and abbreviation. Style means that the appearance, such as upper case or camelback case, is consistent with standard practices.

7. **How well has the model been arranged for readability?** Here we ensure the data model is easy to read. This question is not the most important of the ten categories. However, if your model is hard to read, you may not accurately address the more important categories on the scorecard. Placing parent entities above their child entities, displaying related entities together, and minimizing relationship line length all improve model readability.

8. **How good are the definitions?** Here we ensure the definitions are clear, complete, and correct. Clarity means that a reader can

understand the meaning of a term by reading the definition only once. Completeness means that the definition is at the appropriate level of detail and that it includes all the necessary components such as derivations, synonyms, exceptions, and examples. Correctness means that the definition completely matches what the term means and is consistent with the rest of the business.

9. **How consistent is the model with the enterprise?** Here we ensure the structures on the data model are represented in a broad and consistent context, so that one set of terminology and rules can be spoken in the organization. Ideally we would compare the data model being reviewed with an enterprise data model.

10. **How well does the metadata match the data?** Here we confirm the model and the actual data that will be stored within the resulting structures are consistent with each other. Does the column **Customer_Last_Name** really contain the customer's last name, for example? The Data category is designed to reduce these surprises and help ensure the structures on the model match the data these structures will be holding.

Following is an example of an actual Scorecard report I created based on a recent data model review:

#	Category	Total score	Model score	%	Comments
1.	How well does the model capture the requirements?	15	14	93%	Revisit some AKs
2.	How complete is the model?	15	15	100%	Legacy system mapping
3.	How well does the model match its scheme?	10	10	100%	Lots of processing attributes
4.	How structurally sound is the model?	15	10	66%	Null AKs
5.	How well does the model leverage generic structures?	10	10	100%	Perfect use of abstraction
6.	How well does the model follow naming standards?	5	4	80%	Great standard for table naming
7.	How well has the model been arranged for readability?	5	4	80%	Incorporate a conceptual data model

#	Category	Total score	Model score	%	Comments
8.	How good are the definitions?	10	9	90%	Very comprehensive definitions
9.	How consistent is the model with the enterprise?	5	5	100%	Great rapport with business
10.	How well does the metadata match the data?	10	10	100%	Handles changing natural account numbers
	TOTAL SCORE	100	91		

The model that was reviewed in this example received a score of 91. I share this Scorecard report with you because 91 is the highest score I have ever given in a data model review. I believe that lower scores tend to stimulate action. Nobody wants to get a low score, so a low score traditionally receives a rapid response and the model is quickly corrected along with a request to rescore. For example, if someone gives you a data model to review that is missing definitions and you give the model zero in the definitions category, you will most likely get a very quick response from the modeler saying the definitions will arrive shortly. It is good to be a strict grader, as the end result is a higher quality data model and therefore a higher quality application!

Note on this report that category 4 was a strong area for improvement and categories 6 and 7 also contain areas for improvement. There was a 50 page document that accompanied this Scorecard. This document explained the results in detail. Both strengths and areas for improvement were explained in detail through a complete set or representative set of examples. For example, Category 4 lost points because this model was missing some alternate keys. In the accompanying document, those entities missing alternate keys were listed as well as those entities with suspect alternate keys.

You can use the Scorecard on any of your projects—it is not proprietary. In fact, I would love every organization on the planet to use the Scorecard! Here is the reference to include:

DMM Context[2]

The Data Management Maturity (DMM)[SM] Model is a comprehensive reference model of best practices for fundamental data management capabilities. The DMM defines specific capabilities that constitute a gradated path to maturity: establishing, building, sustaining, and optimizing the management of data assets throughout the data lifecycle, from creation through delivery, maintenance, and archiving.

The DMM is organized into a set of processes—6 major Categories, 20 data management Process Areas, and 5 supporting Process Areas—that are applicable to all industries and the model is technology and vendor neutral. While it defines the requirements and activities for effective data management at the organization level, it is not prescriptive about <u>how</u> an organization achieves these capabilities. The DMM allows organizations to evaluate themselves against documented best practices, determine gaps, and improve management of data assets across functional, line of business, and geographic boundaries.

The DMM was collaboratively developed by an author team of over 50 data management experts, IT professionals, and line of business representatives.

---

[2] This section is copyright CMMI Institute with rights granted to Technics Publications to use and reproduce in any format or location where this book is represented or available for sale.

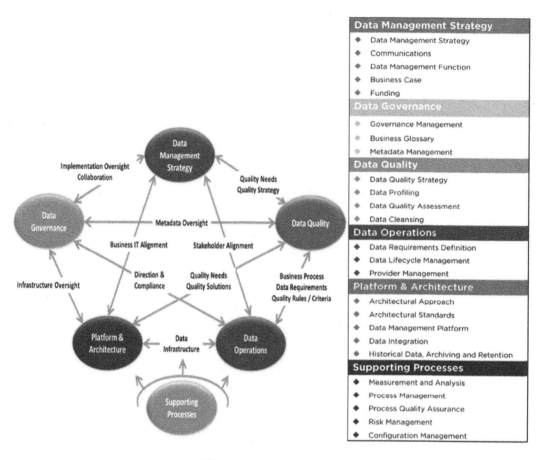

The Process Areas and incremental capability measurement criteria (practice statements) are derived from tested and proven activities that are required to achieve and sustain effective management of an organization's data assets. It contains over 320 specific practices and over 520 example work products that provide evidence of capability and stability. The DMM enables an organization to quickly assess the state of its current capabilities and identify areas for improvement. It is a practical framework that fosters alignment of:

- Vision and strategy
- Implementation of governance mechanisms
- Defining dependencies
- Managing operational components
- Integrating with IT capabilities
- Ensuring data quality

- Developing shared data resources
- Incorporating trusted data into the organization's data stores.

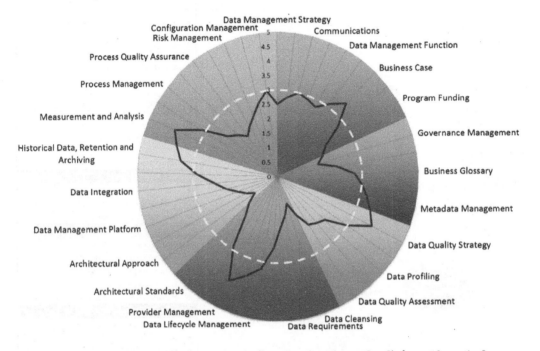

The model's overall goals are to help organizations to improve proficiency in management of their critical data assets, to gain the benefits of a well-planned data management program, and to provide a measurement standard supporting continuous improvement, compliance, and audit readiness.

A complete training and certification program supports organizations and data management professionals in realizing the business benefits of data management maturity. More information can be found at http://cmmiinstitute.com/data-management-maturity.

DMM AND DATA MODELING

The data modeling-centric view of the DMM, illustrated below, corresponds to data modeling's historical role in the data management industry.

Data Modeling Integration with DMM Process Areas[3]

It was data modeling that initiated a slowly growing but powerful trend to capture meaningful metadata, gain agreement on business terms, establish governance for shared data, and extend design of individual data stores to integrated designs for shared repositories, etc. The evolution of data modeling and its embedding in both IT and business processes has resulted in:

- Continuously improving data modeling processes

- Sharpened focus on the strategic long-term effort of developing a robust and resilient data layer

---

[3] The size of the circles have no meaning, it is just to fit the text in the boxes.

- A corresponding and obvious need for standards and compliance processes

- Increased understanding and adoption of business engagement in data architecture.

The achievements of data modelers over the past decades have been a solid foundation for transforming the thinking of the data management industry. This common language has enabled organizations to address the challenge of creating well-planned and executed data management programs.

Data modeling is not addressed in the DMM as a separate Process Area for two reasons:

- The DMM author team considers data modeling to be a fully mature discipline as its methods and best practices have been applied and enhanced for 40 years since Dr. Peter Chen (our Carnegie Mellon DMM Faculty Advisor) invented entity-relationship modeling in 1975.

- Once business stakeholders have approved terms, values, and relationships in the logical model, their further engagement is limited; it is an IT function for the data designer to transform it to a physical model. The DMM's process areas are aimed at unifying the perspective, language, and vision of IT, data management, and the lines of business to further the goal of increased understanding of business responsibilities for the data created and managed. Therefore, by design, it does not focus on topics that are primarily technical in nature.

However, since data models and modeling form the conceptual backbone for almost all data management disciplines, they are referenced in many DMM Process Areas. For example, practice statement 1.2 in Business Glossary states:

Functional Practice Statement

1.2   Logical data models are created with reference to defined and approved business terms.

When standard approved business terms exist, they should be referenced to derived attribute names. This practice prevents the creation of nonstandard terms by each project effort. It is implemented in physical data stores, project by project, and supports the objective of clarifying and improving business usage versus adding complexity. Business terms are the basis for facts (attributes) about an entity although naming conventions and database design practices may result in altered naming (e.g., the standard industry practice of ending each attribute name with a classword). For example, a business term describing a pension plan may be "Date of Plan Origination"; the corresponding logical name may be "Plan Origination Date."

Throughout the DMM, there are a number of dependencies both to and from data modeling. The headings below address each Process Area spoke in the diagram, followed by a statement of its purpose and brief highlights of key dependencies with data models and data modeling.

Data Management Function: *Provides leadership and structure for implementing data management principles and best practices across the organization. It serves as knowledge-based continuity for enterprise data and for persistent products and services needed to ensure the quality and shareability of enterprise data assets.*

However it may be structured within a specific organization, the data management function provides permanent and critical infrastructure support for foundational and persistent processes, standards, and products. Examples of products includes an enterprise data model, metadata repository, or business glossary—products that have far-reaching impacts for many stakeholders. Processes typically include core compliance functions for data representation standards, data access standards, etc.

Governance Management: *Establishing a structure to implement collaborative decision making and oversight of the data management program and to assign ownership, stewardship, and executive responsibilities for enterprise data.*

"Enterprise data" refers to data assets that are logically shared. As capabilities are strengthened, governance responsibilities should, over time, be delineated by subject areas. Subject areas are anchored by core entity types, a central concept in data modeling. A significant portion of governance activities are substantially related to data meaning, data values, data naming, and metadata, etc.

Business Glossary: *An approved, governed compendium of approved business terms and definitions, which creates common understanding, enables efficient data sharing and controls, and supports business processes and decisions.*

The development of agreed upon business terms is prior to the development of logical data models. However, in many organizations development of approved shared terms and definitions has frequently been accomplished directly through data modeling efforts. It is often the case that the models have come first, and business term lists are later developed from entity types and attributes. The DMM emphasizes the development of business terms with approved standards and by governance but refers to entity type and attribute names and business line-specific term lists as consumable sources.

Metadata Management: *Identifies, describes, and provides content, context, structure, and classifications pertaining to the organization's data assets for effective usage, retrieval, and traceability.*

Effective metadata management—business, technical, and operational—requires approved categories, properties, standards, and a metamodel that meets the needs of the business and IT. Sound modeling practices require the unambiguous specification of metadata and its properties for data at rest as well as source to target mapping for data in motion. The DMM specifies that with increased capabilities, metadata needs to accurately reflect the implemented data architecture including mapping from business terms to logical names to physical names and data stores. Metadata implementation phases are recommended to be prioritized by subject areas.

Data Quality Assessment: *A systematic, business-driven approach to measure and evaluate data quality according to processes, employing data quality rules, is established and followed.*

The lines of business must determine the quality characteristics of the data they create and manage: fitness for purpose, the degree to which defects are acceptable (thresholds), and the desired state (targets). The DMM advocates establishing data quality requirements by subject area, employing data quality dimensions, and starting with critical data sets: master data, other highly shared data, or core data attributes, e.g., those vital for mandatory reporting. Modeling metadata, such as allowed values and ranges, are substantive sources for development or derivation of data quality rules.

Data Profiling: *The organization has developed a comprehensive understanding of the content, quality, and rules of specified data sets under management.*

In conducting data profiling, a discovery task to evaluate if, and how, physical records diverge from expected characteristics—referential integrity, nulls in mandatory columns, allowed values diverging from documented metadata, etc.—data models and associated metadata are a critical source of reference for determining defects. The DMM requires traceability between data requirements, documented metadata, quality rules, and physical data models.

Data Cleansing: *The organization has developed and uses mechanisms, predefined rules, processes, and techniques to validate and correct data and uses the results to augment quality rules and improve business processes.*

Defects detected through the data profiling and data quality assessment processes, including root cause analysis at or close to the point of origin, may cause modifications to data store designs. Remediation is required to be prioritized by business needs and ensure that the same data sets are not repeatedly cleansed in multiple sources, pointing to the need for a well-architected data layer and application of best practices for data store designs.

Data Requirements Definition: *Establishes the process used to identify, precisely define, prioritize, document, and validate the data needed to achieve business objectives.*

The requirements development process within the systems development lifecycle is typically standardized and followed in most organizations. However, the data requirements process often has gaps; for instance, compliance processes do not always check for alignment of requirements for application actions with the logical data model for the corresponding data store.

The DMM specifies that: "**2.4 Data requirements are aligned with the corresponding data model(s) and other related artifacts.** *A best practice is to develop the logical data model in parallel with supporting analyses that* *decompose business requirements into finer granularity and eventually into atomic testable statements. The logical design is iteratively refined, corresponding with requirements refinement. Other artifacts may include work products such as custom-to-COTS mapping, etc."* It further specifies that the overall organization's requirements process includes compliance requirements for data specifications and metadata.

Data Lifecycle Management: *The definition of data usage and dependencies across business processes for data that is critical for an important business function or needed by multiple business processes, enabling control of the organization's data flows throughout the data lifecycle from creation or acquisition to retirement.*

The DMM requires that in-scope business processes that create and update data, such as those processes used by multiple business areas, are mapped to the data representations at the model, entity type, and attribute level and then at the physical level. This effort is prioritized and requires the mutual agreement of business experts and data architects; it enables traceability of data across the lifecycle, accurate impact analysis, and improved business processes and strengthens data ownership and stewardship.

Architectural Standards: *An approved set of expectations for governing architectural elements supporting data representations, data access, and data distribution, which are fundamental to data asset control and the efficient use and exchange of information.*

The DMM takes the position that standards are essential: they support evolution toward the target data architecture, assure controlled access, simplify the development lifecycle, and govern data distribution. Standards for data models and metadata are emphasized as well as a robust and effective compliance process to ensure that standards are followed across the organization. Among other key data standards referenced are those for data access, data provisioning, and data security.

Data Integration: *Data integration addresses data transport and processing from multiple sources (connecting, combining, transforming, de-duplication, etc.) into a destination environment to improve data availability for business processes that require data consolidation and aggregation such as analytics.*

Effective data integration across an organization requires standard processes and rules for consolidating data and compliance with standards for data representation. The modeler is the designer of the consolidated data store employing approved business terms as well as applying naming and metadata standards. The DMM requires source identification, source to target mapping, and application of standard practices and techniques for relational, dimensional, or non-relational models of the target destination.

DMBOK CONTEXT

The DAMA Data Management Body of Knowledge (DAMA-DMBOK or DMBOK for short), is the definitive standard for the data management industry. Below is the DAMA-DMBOK2 Knowledge Wheel, containing all of the facets of data management with data governance at its core. We can see that data modeling is one of the important facets.

Copyright © 2014 by DAMA International   4

---

[4] DAMA International. (2016). Data Modeling. In *The DAMA Guide to the Data Management Body of Knowledge (DAMA-DMBOK)* (2nd ed.). Basking Ridge, New Jersey: Technics Publications.

In addition, within DMBOK2 there are contexts diagrams for each of these facets. The following figure contains the data modeling context diagram, and we can see that one of the key technical drivers is data model validation measurements—one example being the Data Model Scorecard, which is referenced in DMBOK2.

Data Modeling

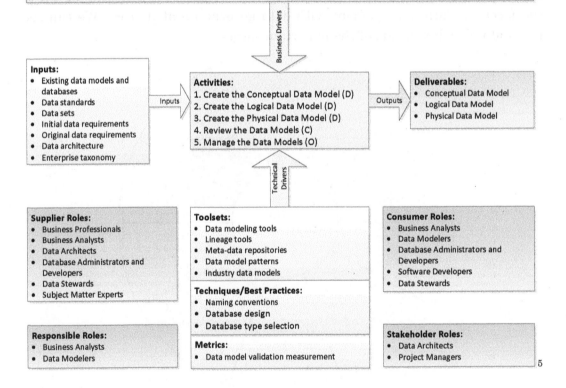

Definition: Data modeling is the process of discovering, analyzing, and scoping data requirements, and then representing and communicating these data requirements in a precise form called the "data model". Often, the Conceptual Data Model (CDM) is created first, followed by the Logical Data Model (LDM), followed by the Physical Data Model (PDM). There can be iteration between these levels (e.g. a change to an LDM can trigger a change to a CDM), and sometimes the PDM is created first.

Goal: To confirm and document our understanding of different perspectives, which leads to applications that more closely align with current and future business requirements, and creates a foundation to successfully complete broad-scoped initiatives such as master data management and data governance programs.

Business Drivers

Inputs:
- Existing data models and databases
- Data standards
- Data sets
- Initial data requirements
- Original data requirements
- Data architecture
- Enterprise taxonomy

Inputs

Activities:
1. Create the Conceptual Data Model (D)
2. Create the Logical Data Model (D)
3. Create the Physical Data Model (D)
4. Review the Data Models (C)
5. Manage the Data Models (O)

Outputs

Deliverables:
- Conceptual Data Model
- Logical Data Model
- Physical Data Model

Technical Drivers

Supplier Roles:
- Business Professionals
- Business Analysts
- Data Architects
- Database Administrators and Developers
- Data Stewards
- Subject Matter Experts

Responsible Roles:
- Business Analysts
- Data Modelers

Toolsets:
- Data modeling tools
- Lineage tools
- Meta-data repositories
- Data model patterns
- Industry data models

Techniques/Best Practices:
- Naming conventions
- Database design
- Database type selection

Metrics:
- Data model validation measurement

Consumer Roles:
- Business Analysts
- Data Modelers
- Database Administrators and Developers
- Software Developers
- Data Stewards

Stakeholder Roles:
- Data Architects
- Project Managers

5

5 DAMA International. (2016). Data Modeling. In *The DAMA Guide to the Data Management Body of Knowledge (DAMA-DMBOK)* (2nd ed.). Basking Ridge, New Jersey: Technics Publications.

From DMBOK2: *Just like other areas of IT, continuous improvement practices should be deployed, and techniques such as time to value, support costs, and data model quality validators such as the Data Model Scorecard® (Hoberman 2009), can all be used to validate the model for correctness, completeness, and consistency.*[6]

---

[6] DAMA International. (2016). Data Modeling. In *The DAMA Guide to the Data Management Body of Knowledge (DAMA-DMBOK)* (2nd ed.). Basking Ridge, New Jersey: Technics Publications.

In this section we will go into detail into each of the ten categories of the Data Model Scorecard:

- Chapter 4: Correctness
- Chapter 5: Completeness
- Chapter 6: Scheme
- Chapter 7: Structure
- Chapter 8: Abstraction
- Chapter 9: Standards
- Chapter 10: Readability
- Chapter 11: Definitions
- Chapter 12: Consistency
- Chapter 13: Data

In this section we will go into detail into each of the ten categories of the Data Model Scorecard.

Chapter 4
Category One: Correctness
How well does the model capture the requirements?

The "Correctness" category checks that the data model captures what the requirements need it to capture. For example, if a manufacturing company is building a new inventory reporting system and a key requirement is to report on daily inventory levels for each product, does the data model contain the structures that would allow this report to be produced?

Ideally we would grade this category by sitting at our desk with a thick, comprehensive set of requirements on one part of our desk and the data model we are reviewing on the other part of our desk and go through each requirement and make sure everything appears on the data model correctly.

In practice, though, how often do we receive comprehensive requirements? Usually, if we are lucky enough to receive any requirements, they tend to be light and often in the form of short user stories (short statements in the form of "As <u>who</u>, I want <u>what</u> for <u>why</u>."). At times we receive no requirements and have to rely on the data modeling process to uncover requirements. At other times, requirements can be conflicting such as something documented that appears at odds with what a knowledgeable business expert just raised in a requirements workshop. What complicates abridged and conflicting requirements is the reality that requirements change over time; what was a high-priority requirement this week may be replaced by a completely different high-priority requirement next week.

CATEGORY EXPECTATIONS

This section contains a subset of what to look for to grade the Correctness category. In these days of iterative development (e.g. agile), it is unlikely there will be an in-depth requirements document we can read to ensure all of the requirements are represented correctly on the data model. Instead, I look for evidence that requirements work was performed and then compare this documentation with the data model. Documentation most commonly takes the form of interview write-ups, user stories, reports or forms, database or interface layouts, and through prototypes. I will show examples of each of these using the following model for an application that captures survey results, called Survey Data Entry (SDE).

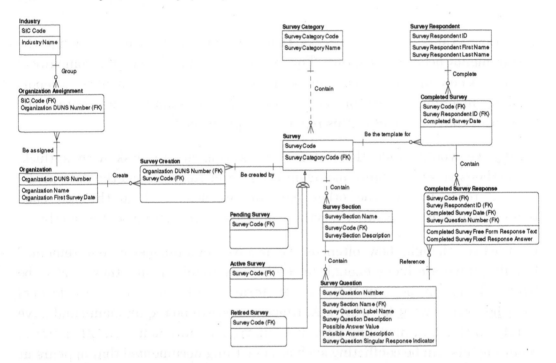

This model needs to capture the data requirements for a survey data entry application. **Organizations** operate in many different **Industries** and create **Surveys** across many different **Categories** such as Consumer Satisfaction or Market Research. Each **Survey** goes through a lifecycle (**Pending**, **Active**, or **Retired**) and contains **Sections**. Within each **Section** there are **Questions**. A **Survey Respondent** may complete a survey, which includes answers to each of the survey questions.

> *Look for evidence that interviews were performed, and compare this evidence to the data model.*

An interview is a systematic approach designed to elicit information from a person or group of people in an informal or formal setting by asking relevant questions and documenting the responses. When grading the correctness category, I look for evidence that the modeler spoke with business professionals and business analysts to make sure the requirements are understood. This evidence could be a summary of an interview in a document template format or even a recording of the interview.

Once I know that at least one interview took place with the right audience, I can then read or listen to the results of the interview to make sure the model correctly incorporated those requirements specified in the interview.

For example, here is paragraph from an interview summary with Bob Jones, the senior business analyst for the SDE project:

> We need to be able to have a pool of questions we can reuse across surveys. A question such as "How was your stay?" is something that multiple hotels would be interested in. Reusing questions will create greater consistency across surveys and also allow the survey creator to build surveys in less time because he or she can just choose the questions they would like instead of creating them from scratch each time like we are doing today...

Note that based upon this interview summary, our model will need to change. Currently, a **Survey Question** must belong to one **Survey Section,** which belongs to one **Survey**. We need to update the model to allow the **Survey Question** to belong to multiple **Surveys** instead of just one.

Look for evidence that user stories were created, and compare this evidence to the data model.

A user story is a description consisting of one or more sentences in simple terms like "As <u>who</u>, I want <u>what</u> for <u>why</u>." A user story captures what a user currently does or would like to do. User stories are popular forms of requirements on agile development teams. In our SDE project, here is an example of a user story:

> As the Survey Data Governance Lead, I want questions that are ratings-based to have a fixed set of choices for improving data quality and data analytics. For example, the question "How was your stay?" should only allow the numbers one through five,

where one is poor and five is excellent. It should not allow the survey respondent to enter a zero or six.

Note that based upon this user story, our model will need to change. Currently, we do not have a structure to restrict the answer set for ratings-based questions. We can recommend adding a **Rating Type** entity, which will categorize each question and contain a category for those questions that are ratings-based.

Look for evidence that reports or forms were analyzed, and compare this evidence to the data model.

For operational applications it can be very useful to analyze data entry forms, and for reporting systems analyzing reports can prove useful. For our SDE model, for example, here is a sample survey form:

COMMENT CARD

Server _____ Date _____

At Publyk House, we want you to have a truly enjoyable and memorable experience each time you visit our restaurant. Please take a moment to share your comments, suggestions or questions about our food, service and ambiance. Your comments are intended for private use to make your experience as enjoyable as possible.

Were you greeted properly?
POOR ☐ ☐ ☐ ☐ ☐ EXCELLENT

How was your server?
POOR ☐ ☐ ☐ ☐ ☐ EXCELLENT

How was the atmosphere?
POOR ☐ ☐ ☐ ☐ ☐ EXCELLENT

How was the price/value?
POOR ☐ ☐ ☐ ☐ ☐ EXCELLENT

What is your favorite menu item & your least favorite? Why? _____
_____
_____

How did you hear about us? _____

Do you plan on coming back? ☐ Yes ☐ No

Would you recommend us to a friend? ☐ Yes ☐ No

If you would like to receive promotional e-mails, including new menu items, please write down your email address:
_____

Your comments: _____
_____
_____
_____

Notice that some of the questions on our surveys may contain questions that allow for more than one response. A question such as "What is your favorite menu item & your least favorite? Why?" can have multiple responses. The model we are reviewing currently only allows for at most one text response or at most one fixed response for each question (see the **Completed Survey Response** entity).

Look for evidence that database or interface layouts were analyzed, and compare this evidence to the data model.

For example, if the survey application we are designing is based on an old legacy system, we can study the legacy structures to make sure we have all of the requirements. Imagine this is the legacy structure for **Survey Respondent** for example:

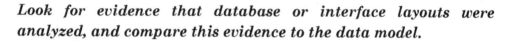

SurveyRes	
Field Name	**Data Type**
ID	AutoNumber
FName	Text
MName	Text
LName	Text
BDate	Date/Time

We can see here, assuming that **MName** is the middle name and **BDate** is the birthdate, that middle name and birthdate should be considered for addition to our **Survey Respondent** entity.

Look for evidence that a prototype was built, and compare this evidence to the data model.

Prototyping is a concrete means of identifying, describing, and validating relational and dimensional requirements. There are some very easy to use tools available to create prototypes, such as Excel® and Balsamiq®. Balsamiq is a very user-friendly way to create screen mock-ups (see www.balsamiq.com for more details).

A horizontal prototype models a shallow and possibly wide view of the system's functionality. It typically does not have any business logic running behind the visualization. A vertical prototype models a deep and usually small subset of the entire system's functionality.

For example, as part of a survey prototype, we built this Survey Status drop-down that was approved by the business:

| Survey Lifecycle: |
| Pending |
| Approved |
| Active |
| Retired |

We notice on the data model we are reviewing that there are only three subtypes: **Pending**, **Active**, and **Retired**. Approved appears in this prototype but not as a subtype on the model.

━━ ━━ ━━ ━━ ━━

Check to make sure the right scope was chosen.

We need to make sure the data model we are reviewing chose the right scope at a general level, either project or program.

Project scope means we can ignore the rest of the business and just focus on a particular department or small section of the business. If the team wants to call it **Client** and we know the rest of the organization calls it **Customer**, we can still call it **Client** with a project scope.

Program efforts require agreeing on consistent names and definitions and rules. If the team wants to call it **Client** and we know the rest of the organization calls it **Customer**, we will need to call it **Customer** with a program scope.

So for example, if we are building a survey application for a single hotel within a large hotel chain, this application's data model will most likely have project scope. Terms can be used that are specific to this particular hotel without concern for how the other hotels view this same information. However, if this survey application will be used by the entire hotel chain, we have program scope and need to make sure the data model supports the perspective of the entire hotel chain.

Check to make sure the right time perspective was chosen.

A model can represent how a business works today or how a business might work sometime in the future. A model with the "as is" perspective captures how the business works today. If there are archaic business rules, they will appear on this model even if the business is planning on modifying them in the near future. A model with the "to be" perspective can represent any time period in the future. Whether end of the year, five years out, or ten years out, a "to be" perspective represents an ideal view of the organization. When a model needs to support an organization's vision or strategic view, a "to be" perspective is preferred. Note that most organizations who need a "to be" perspective first have to build an "as is" perspective to create a starting point.

If we are modeling the current ordering process, we would expect the data model to capture the "as is" perspective. If we are building a data model for a proposed data warehouse that does not exist today, we would expect the "to be" perspective.

Check to make sure the right language was chosen.

Are we modeling the business language or the application language? The business language uses business terminology and rules. It does not matter whether the organization is using a vendor package or internally-built application; the business will be represented in business concepts. The application language uses application terminology and rules. It is a view of the business through the eyes of an application. If the application uses the term **Object** instead of the term **Product**, it will appear as **Object** on the model and be defined according to how the application defines the term, not how the business defines it.

For general guidelines, if we are driving development from requirements, we choose the business language. If we are driving development from an existing system and reverse engineering is an important part of the project, than an application language is chosen.

I once had to build a data model of a subset of a large vendor package, SAP. While building the data model, I encountered the term "characteristic." I have never heard this term before, and after doing some research, I learned that the business counterpart for the term "characteristic" was "classification." I now had to decide whether to use the term "characteristic" or "classification." Because I was driving development from an existing system, I chose the application language and went with "characteristic."

Check to make sure the model adheres to industry standards.

One of the straightforward correctness issues to catch is an attribute with a length or format different than the industry standard: a five-character Social Security number, a six-character phone number, or an 18-character email address. This is a best practice that can be identified without much knowledge of the content of the model.

Confirm stakeholder signoff on the model.

I like to see evidence that the person or group that the data model was built for has approved the model. This can be as simple as a signature or an email message saying "I approve, let's move on." Stakeholder approval does more than just provide model credibility. It also means that the reviewers who are also stakeholders will take the review much more seriously and be more supportive of the resulting design.

One of the challenges the modeler may face during the review process is that sometimes the modeler will encounter a person or group who needs to validate the data model but does not want to see the actual data model diagram. In these situations, the modeler needs to get creative on how to validate the model, often using other mediums such as reports, business assertions, or prototypes.

For example, if the reviewer does not want to see this model they need to approve:

They can instead show the reviewer these business assertions:

- Each **Author** may write one or many **Titles**.
- Each **Title** must be written by one or many **Authors**.

Once the reviewer has approved these assertions, they can approve the model. If the reviewer finds faults in the assertions, the model can be updated and the updated assertions shown to the reviewer for approval.

Summary of Correctness Checks

✓ Look for evidence that interviews were performed, and compare this evidence to the data model.

✓ Look for evidence that user stories were created, and compare this evidence to the data model.

✓ Look for evidence that reports or forms were analyzed, and compare this evidence to the data model.

✓ Look for evidence that database or interface layouts were analyzed, and compare this evidence to the data model.

✓ Look for evidence that a prototype was built, and compare this evidence to the data model.

✓ Check to make sure the right scope was chosen.

✓ Check to make sure the right time perspective was chosen.

✓ Check to make sure the right language was chosen.

✓ Check to make sure the model adheres to industry standards.

✓ Confirm stakeholder signoff on the model.

Chapter 5
Category Two: Completeness
How complete is the model?

The "Completeness" category checks two areas: completeness of requirements and completeness of metadata.

Completeness of requirements means that all of the requirements requested appear on the data model and nothing extra. "Nothing extra" means we catch structures added to the data model that were not mentioned in the requirements. There might have been structures added "for future use" to the data model, but if these structures were not explicitly asked for in the requirements, are they really needed? There is a very good chance these extras will become part of the requirements, but if this is the case, the project plan will need to be adjusted. Try not to give "freebies"! The little extras we include thinking they are valuable often come back to haunt us later on during development and testing.

Completeness of metadata means that all of the descriptive information surrounding the model is captured. For example, if we are reviewing a physical data model, we would expect the formatting and length of each attribute to appear on the model. If we are reviewing a logical data model, we would expect full business names of each attribute. And if we are reviewing a conceptual data model, we would expect definitions for each of the key terms.

CATEGORY EXPECTATIONS

This section contains a subset of what to look for to grade the Completeness category.

Confirm business metadata captured.

Business metadata includes all of the descriptive information surrounding the model that would be useful for business professionals and business analysts. An organization needs to define the checklist of required business metadata for each level of model such as the examples below:

- Definitions
- Business purpose
- Examples of a real-world instance of the entity or attribute
- Data governance
- Model name
- Model create date
- Model last update date.

Confirm technical metadata captured.

Technical metadata includes all of the descriptive information surrounding the model that would be useful for IT professionals. An organization needs to define the checklist of required technical metadata for each level of model, similar to what appears below:

- File name
- Model version
- Schema namespace
- Names of tables, attributes, indexes, and constraints
- Attribute nullability. Nullability is a setting which determines whether the attribute is mandatory (NOT NULL) or optional (NULL). Note that some attributes may be conditionally nullable depending on values of other attributes; this should be documented and can be enforced by database constraints.
- Domain limits (e.g., min/max or list of allowed values)
- Computed (i.e., derived) fields
- Volumetrics (i.e., initial data volumes and expected increases in the amount of data, expected rates of change, etc.)
- Attribute formatting and length.

- Source information. This includes the system name, field name, description, data type, length, and formatting of each source attribute. A source attribute is an attribute whose data will eventually be loaded into one or more attributes on our data model. Source information also includes transformation logic for derived attributes. So for example, if one of our attributes is **Gross Sales Amount**, the source information would include metadata for each component of this derived attribute such as **List Price** and **Sales Quantity**.

Confirm each requirement is completely captured.

The data model must capture all of the necessary structures for each requirement. For example, if there is a requirement to view the complete customer profile, we would raise a concern if **Customer Last Name** is missing from the customer profile data model. Notice how the Completeness category differs from the prior category on Correctness. Correctness includes ensuring all of the requirements are on the model; Completeness includes ensuring we have all of the necessary structures for each requirement.

Confirm no freebies given.

We should evaluate the costs and benefits of structures on the data model that were not explicitly requested in the requirements. Sometimes the modeler might include structures that he or she believes will be needed in the future. I like to catch any of these extraneous structures and challenge the modeler as to why they are included. It is always easy to add a few structures on the diagram, but it can be a lot harder to implement them. If there is a strong case for keeping them on the model, the requirements need to expand to include them as well. This can lead to be giving additional time or money to complete the project.

For example, assume we are reviewing the data model on the next page:

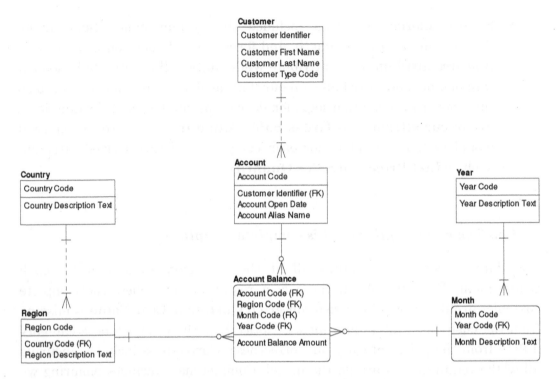

On this dimensional data model, the granularity of **Account Balance Amount** is **Region**, **Month**, and **Account**. Yet what if the requirements only specified **Account Balance Amount** by **Region**, **Month**, and **Customer**? We would not need to have **Account** on the model. I would challenge the modeler as to why **Account** was added. If the business feels it would be an important requirement, then **Account** should make its way into the requirements as well.

Confirm ambiguous requirements clarified.

Often requirements documents contain sentences or sections that can be interpreted more than one way. For example, a common phrase I notice in requirements documents is "I want to see all of the details." But what does "all of the details" really mean? The details need to be specified including listing all of the attributes needed as part of this requirement.

Summary of Completeness Checks

✓ Confirm business metadata captured.

✓ Confirm technical metadata captured.

✓ Confirm each requirement is completely captured.

✓ Confirm no freebies given.

✓ Confirm ambiguous requirements clarified.

Chapter 6
Category Three: Scheme
How well does the model match its scheme?

The "Scheme" category checks that the data model we are reviewing matches our expectation for its scheme. The scheme includes level of detail (conceptual, logical, and physical), and also whether relational, dimensional, or NoSQL. For example, if we are reviewing a conceptual data model that has characteristics of a physical data model such as attribute formatting and nullability, we would catch it in this category. There are currently five cells covering ten schemes as shown in the following table:

	Relational	Dimensional
Conceptual	Broad scope concepts and rules	Broad scope metrics and slicing
Logical	Normalized	All metrics and levels shown
Physical	Relational, Dimensional, Column, Key-Value, Document, Graph	

There are conceptual and logical models that can be both relational and dimensional, giving us four schemes shown above in the four separate cells. The remaining six schemes (shown in the fifth cell) are all physical and include the traditional relational and dimensional schemes as well as the four most popular NoSQL schemes: Column, Key-Value, Document, and Graph.

Each data model should fit into one of these ten schemes. I once reviewed these categories with the IT department at a bank and they told me that their models were not logical, they were not physical—they were "physio-logical"! They didn't have time to do separate logical and physical data models so they did one model to try to capture both. This type of model would get a zero in this category, as it does not fit cleanly into one of the five cells.

In this chapter, we will cover the expectations for conceptual, logical, and physical data models, and within each of these sections we will cover both relational and dimensional variations. For physical data models, we will also briefly cover NoSQL (in addition to relational and dimensional). Before jumping into the category expectations, let's briefly explain each scheme. For a more thorough explanation of each scheme, please refer to my book *Data Modeling Made Simple*.

A conceptual data model is a concise data model that captures the business need and scope of the application in terms of concepts. A concept is a key idea that is both *basic* and *critical* to your *audience*. "Basic" means this term is probably mentioned many times a day in conversations with the people who are the audience for the model, which includes the people who need to validate the model as well as the people who need to use the model. "Critical" means the business would be very different or non-existent without this concept. "Audience" refers to the users of the model. If there are different types of audiences, where some require more detail than others, you may find yourself building more than one conceptual data model.

A logical data model is a detailed data model that contains all of the structures required for the business solution to an application. The logical data model looks the same regardless of whether we are implementing in MongoDB or Oracle. The logical data model is also a great mapping point when multiple technologies exist. The logical data model will show one technology-independent perspective, and then we can map this business perspective to each of the various technology perspectives, similar to a hub in a bicycle tire:

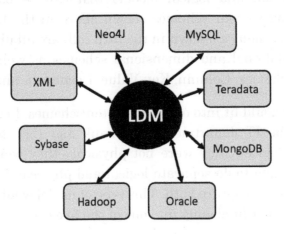

SCHEME | 69

When new technologies come along, we can use the logical data model as a starting point and therefore save an incredible amount of time in building the application, as well as improving consistency within the organization.

The physical data model is the logical data model compromised or augmented to create the detailed technical solution. This is the first time we are actually concerning ourselves with technology and related issues such as performance, storage, and security. An Oracle physical data model will look different from a MongoDB physical data model.

For each conceptual, logical, and physical data model, we need to decide whether we are building a relational or dimensional mindset. This is the thought process we go through in deciding whether we go relational or dimensional:

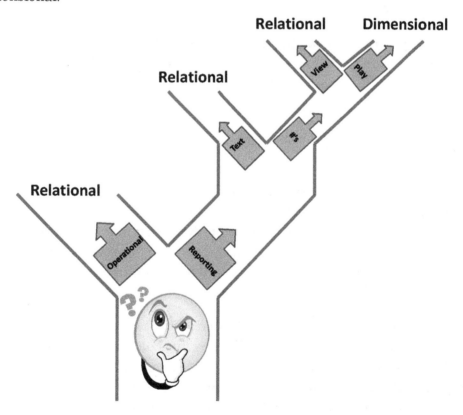

The first decision is whether we are building an operational or reporting system. An operational system automates one or more business processes for an organization such as a claims processing system for an insurance company or an order entry system for a retail organization. A reporting system uses data from one or more operational systems to produce an evaluation of how part or all of the organization is performing. If we are building an operational system, we choose the relational path because relational captures business processes and an operational system automates business processes, so it is a perfect fit. If building a reporting system, continue to the next fork in the road, which is whether there is a requirement to see text or numbers. If the only reporting requirements involve seeing text, such as names, codes, or descriptions, go relational. If there is a need to see numbers, continue to the next fork. The next fork in the road is whether these numbers are view only or going to be played with. If the requirement is just to view the numbers in a static fashion and not do any analysis with them, then go relational. If we are building a reporting system where there is a requirement to analyze quantities or amounts (such as to analyze **Gross Sales Amount** at a month level and then drill down to the date level), then go dimensional.

So, to summarize the decision process whether to go relational or dimensional, the only time we are going to build dimensional data models is when we have a requirement to analyze numbers. For everything else, we go relational.

The facing page contains an example of each scheme, along with a short description in the following paragraphs.

In the relational CDM example, the lines connecting **Customer** with **Account** and **Account** with **Account Balance** are business rules. Each **Account Balance** must belong to one **Account**, for example. Not two, not zero, but one and only one. Each of the boxes **Customer**, **Account**, and **Account Balance** are not logical entities or physical tables, but instead concepts or ideas. The concept **Customer,** for example, may translate into dozens of logical entities or physical structures.

In the dimensional CDM example, the level of detail is similar to the relational CDM example, but the focus is different. The lines on the relational represent business rules—on this model, the lines represent navigation paths. "I want to see **Account Balance** by **Region**, **Account**, and **Month**. Afterwards, I may want to navigate from **Region** to **Country** or from **Month** to **Year**." Each of the boxes, similar to the relational CDM, represent concepts and not logical or physical structures.

SCHEME | 71

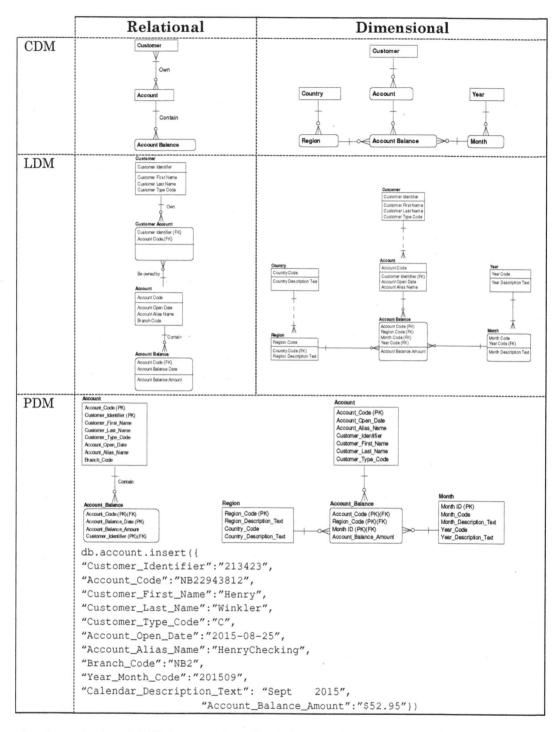

```
db.account.insert({
"Customer_Identifier":"213423",
"Account_Code":"NB22943812",
"Customer_First_Name":"Henry",
"Customer_Last_Name":"Winkler",
"Customer_Type_Code":"C",
"Account_Open_Date":"2015-08-25",
"Account_Alias_Name":"HenryChecking",
"Branch_Code":"NB2",
"Year_Month_Code":"201509",
"Calendar_Description_Text": "Sept    2015",
                "Account_Balance_Amount":"$52.95"})
```

In the relational LDM example, all of the attributes needed for our business solution are present and organized into entities using the technique of normalization. Relational LDMs tend to be very granular, as we can see here with all of the attributes needed to solve the business problem—if the **Branch Code** is needed for an **Account**, it will appear on this model.

In the dimensional LDM example, all of the attributes are present to answer the required business questions. Notice that the dimensional models need to be simple, and if **Branch Code** was not needed to answer a business question but the **Region** the branch resides within is needed, only the **Region** will appear as in this example,. It will be up to the development team to roll up branches to regions to make it simpler to answer the business questions.

At the physical level, the structures vary based on the technology. The most common database technology is still the relational database, and therefore our relational LDM becomes a relational PDM and the structures are compromised using techniques such as denormalization to produce an efficient physical design. This is similar to the dimensional LDM; the hierarchies in a dimensional LDM are often flattened in the physical to create a star schema, a physical design where each dimensional is a single structure—a very simple and speedy structure. Other types of databases, such as those that are document-based, will have a very different physical structure like the sample MongoDB document that appears on the previous page. Physical data models often display database-specific characteristics on the diagram such as nullability (whether an attribute can be empty or not).

CATEGORY EXPECTATIONS

This section contains a subset of what to look for to grade the Scheme category.

CONCEPTUAL DATA MODEL ADHERENCE

All conceptual data models should follow the expectations in this section, plus the additional expectations in the relational or dimensional subsections depending on whether the model is a relational or dimensional data model.

SCHEME | 73

Confirm the conceptual data model captures the business needs and scope of the application.

The most important check for the conceptual is that the model we are reviewing meets the definition for a true conceptual—that is, capturing what the business needs and identifying the scope of the application. If we are building an order entry application, for example, all of the concepts required for order entry should appear on the model. If additional concepts appear, it should be noted on the model that they are out of scope.

Confirm all entities on a conceptual are basic and critical to the audience.

On a conceptual data model, only the most important concepts to your audience should appear. "Basic" meaning that this term is probably mentioned many times a day in normal conversation. "Critical" meaning that the business would be non-existent or completely different without this concept.

Basic and critical (good)	Not basic and not critical (bad)
Customer	Customer Type
Product	Product Color
Employee	Employee Contact Mechanism
Account	Account Status

Catch any attributes on the conceptual, unless the attributes themselves are basic and critical to the audience.

For example, **Phone Number**, although often an attribute, is so important to a communications company that it can be considered a conceptual entity. For a manufacturing company's personnel system, however, **Phone Number** can be considered an attribute and not a conceptual entity.

Make sure many-to-many relationships have not been resolved on a conceptual unless the resolving entity is itself basic and critical to the project.

You do not need to resolve a many-to-many relationship on a conceptual data model.

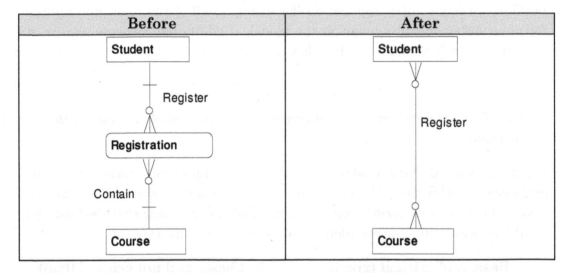

As an aside, however, if resolving the many-to-many relationship leads to another very important entity—if it has relationships to other required entities—then it should be resolved. For example, if **Registration** leads to important **Payment** details, then this many-to-many should be resolved.

Relational Adherence

In addition to the general conceptual data model checks discussed previously, if the conceptual data model you are reviewing is relational, you will also need to apply the checks in this section.

Ensure the relational conceptual data model captures the business needs and scope of the application along with the business rules that exist between the conceptual entities.

We discussed previously the need for the conceptual to capture the business needs and scope of the application. For example, on a relational conceptual data model, each **Customer** may own one or many **Accounts** and each **Account** must be owned by one or many **Customers**. These are business rules and not navigation paths as we would expect on a dimensional.

SCHEME | 75

Ensure each relationship captures the answer to four business questions.

There are four questions that must get answered for each relationship on the conceptual relational, two on participation and two on optionality:

- **Participation**. Participation addresses "one" or "many." That is, for one of the entities participating in a relationship, can it relate to one or many of the other entity participating in the relationship? If, for example, a requirement takes the form of "A **Customer** has **Accounts**," we need to ask the following for participation:
  - Can a **Customer** own more than one **Account**?
  - Can an **Account** be owned by more than one **Customer**?
- **Optionality**. Optionality addresses whether one entity can exist in the absence of the other entity. If, for example, a requirement takes the form of "A **Customer** has **Accounts**," we need to ask the following for optionality:
  - Can a **Customer** exist without an **Account**?
  - Can an **Account** exist without a **Customer**?

Here is a data model I would expect based on the answers to these four business questions:

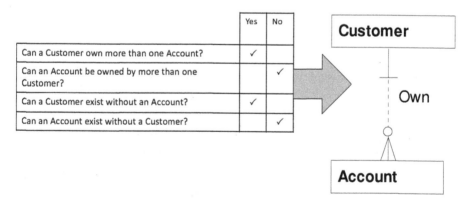

	Yes	No
Can a Customer own more than one Account?	✓	
Can an Account be owned by more than one Customer?		✓
Can a Customer exist without an Account?	✓	
Can an Account exist without a Customer?		✓

Since a **Customer** can own more than one **Account** and can exist without an **Account**, the model contains the cardinality expressing that "Each **Customer** may own one or many **Accounts**." Since an **Account** can only be owned by one **Customer** and cannot exist without a **Customer**, the model contains the cardinality **expressing** that "Each **Account** must be owned by one **Customer**."

Make sure every subtype has one and only one supertype.

A subtype inherits its primary key from its supertype, and therefore a subtype must have the same primary key as its supertype, leading to a subtype having one and only one supertype. What would the primary key of the subtype be if there are two supertypes? For example, on the following diagram, a **Car** is a **Motor Vehicle** and so is identified as a **Motor Vehicle** would be identified. A **House** is a **Dwelling** so would be identified as a **Dwelling** would be identified. But what about **Recreational Vehicle**? Is it a **Motor Vehicle** or a **Dwelling**?

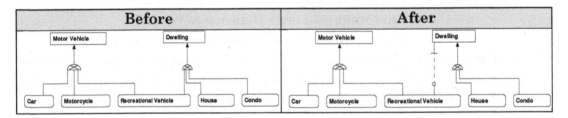

We can recommend the modeler make the weaker supertype/subtype relationship a one-to-one relationship as done in this example. Another option is to create a supertype for **Motor Vehicle** and **Dwelling**, such as **Personal Property**. This way **Personal Property** will have a primary key that will be inherited through all subtypes, so **Recreational Vehicle** will have a single **Personal Property ID**.

Make sure relational modeling is used when needing adhoc reporting.

If there are no business questions yet defined, dimensional models are difficult to build and will constrain the users. If the requirements are "Give me everything" or "I don't know what I want," it is a good practice to model relationally as this way the system has more flexibility.

Dimensional Adherence

In addition to the general conceptual data model checks discussed previously, if the conceptual data model you are reviewing is dimensional, you will also need to apply the checks in this section.

SCHEME | 77

Ensure the dimensional conceptual data model captures the business needs and scope of the application along with the navigation paths required to answer the business questions.

We discussed previously the need for the conceptual to capture the business needs and scope of the application. For example, on a dimensional conceptual data model, we need to view **Account Balance** at different levels of granularity such as by **Region** and **Country**. These are navigation paths and not business rules as we would expect on a relational.

Make sure a dimensional model is built when there is a requirement to analyze measures.

Dimensional models should be built when there is a need to view measures at varying levels of granularity. The reason the dimensional model should be limited to numbers is because its design allows for easy navigation up and down hierarchy levels. For example, a **Gross Sales Amount** of $5 on a particular day might be $150 for the particular month in which that day belongs.

Challenge a dimensional model that is more fine-grained than necessary.

The primary reason we build a dimensional data model is to make it simple to answer business questions. If a dimensional data model is made more fine-grained to answer unforeseen business questions, there could be an impact to the simplicity of the model.

For example, a publisher would like to analyze sales for each of their titles. The requirements process produced the grain matrix on the following page:

	Gross Sales Amount	Net Sales Amount	Books Sold Quantity
Day	x	x	x
Month	x	x	x
Season	x	x	x
Year	x	x	x
Medium	x	x	x
Title	x	x	x
Category	x	x	x
Country	x	x	x
Region	x	x	x
Channel	x	x	x

Here is the dimensional conceptual data model that was produced based upon this grain matrix:

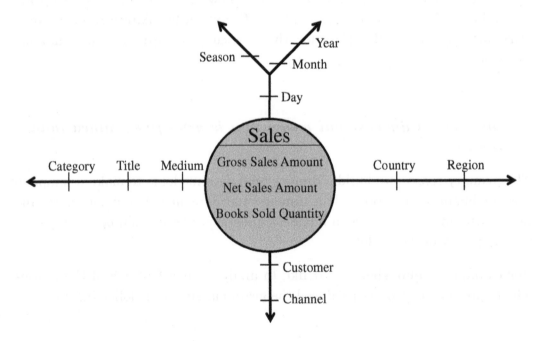

On this data model we see a finer grain than the requirements specified for calendar information—a **Day** level instead of **Month** and **Season**. However, this extra calendar grain was added to increase simplicity (making the model more useable) as it is a much simpler structure to store **Day** level than to

SCHEME | 79

manage **Month** and **Season**, where **Month** and **Season** have separate hierarchy paths. I would not be concerned, therefore, about the increase of calendar grain.

We also notice that **Customer** was added as part of this grain, yet **Customer** was not requested in the grain matrix. We should raise our concern that **Customer** may impact model simplicity because **Customer** was never asked for in the requirements.

LOGICAL DATA MODEL ADHERENCE

All logical data models should follow the expectations in this section, plus the additional expectations in the relational or dimensional subsections depending on whether the model is a relational or dimensional data model.

Ensure the logical data model captures the business solution.

As mentioned with the definition of a logical data model, we need to include everything that will meet the business requirements without complicating the structure with technology (which we will do in the physical). We need to ensure the logical data model contains all of the entities, relationships, and attributes needed to solve the business solution.

Make sure all candidate keys are unique, stable, and mandatory (not null).

Unique means that if there are 100 customers, there will be 100 different **Customer Numbers**. Stable means that the candidate key can never be changed, and mandatory means that there must always be a value and that value cannot be NULL.

Check that many-to-many relationships are resolved on a logical data model.

You need to resolve a many-to-many relationship on a logical data model. The resolution of a many-to-many relationship is called an associative entity. Sometimes associative entities have their own attributes or even relationships too. So **Registration** in this example is the associative entity that resolves the many-to-many relationship between **Student** and **Course** when going from conceptual to logical.

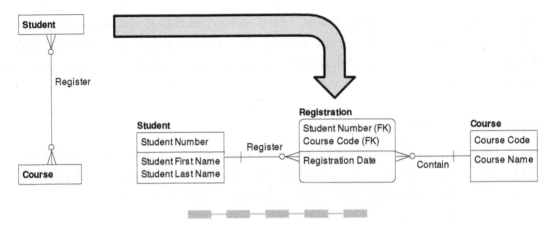

Make sure there are no non-unique indexes on a logical data model.

Secondary keys, also known as non-unique indexes or inversion entries, are added to improve retrieval performance and therefore are part of the technical solution and not part of the business solution. On the following model, we should remove the non-unique indexes on **Student First Name** and **Student Last Name**.

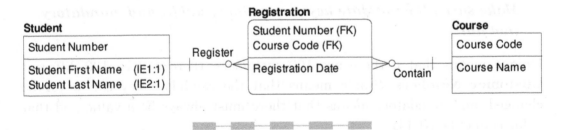

Ensure surrogate keys only appear on a logical data model when new concepts are introduced.

Surrogate keys are added to a logical data model when a new concept has been introduced such as **Party** or **Organization** and a **Party ID** or **Organization ID** must be added as the primary key because no other unique identifier exists for these concepts.

SCHEME | 81

Make sure every entity contains a primary key.

A primary key represents the one or more attributes that uniquely identify an entity instance in an entity and that is chosen to be the unique identifier. The primary key appears "above the line" as in this example:

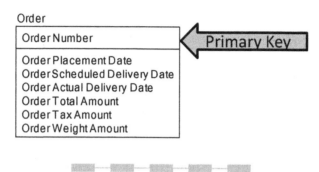

Make sure every relationship has a corresponding foreign key.

A foreign key is an attribute that provides a link to another entity. When a relationship is created between two entities, the entity on the "many" side of the relationship inherits the entire primary key from the entity on the "one" side of the relationship. The foreign key allows for navigation between structures. The foreign key is noted by the initialism "FK":

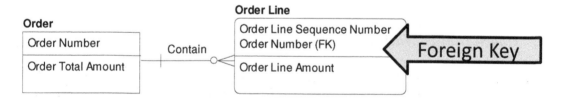

Relational Adherence

In addition to the general logical data model checks discussed previously, if the logical data model you are reviewing is relational, you will also need to apply the checks in this section.

Ensure the relational logical data model captured the business solution, along with the business rules that exist between the logical entities.

As mentioned with the definition of a logical data model, we need to include everything that will meet the business requirements without complicating the structure with technology (which we will do in the physical). In addition, because the model we are reviewing is relational, we would expect the relationship lines to represent detailed rules adhering to the rules of normalization.

Check that multi-valued attributes are separated.

As part of first normal form (1NF), an attribute must contain only one piece of information. Sometimes it is easy to identify attributes that need to be split apart into two or more other attributes, and sometimes it can be more subtle.

An easy example is if both first and last name are stored within **Customer Name**. Where it gets tricky is when the attribute theoretically could be split apart, but does anyone from the business really ever need to see it in separate pieces? This is the important question to ask. **Postal Code** could be multi-valued for example, depending on your perspective of this field. The first digit in the **Postal Code** covers region. The next two digits specify a **Facility** (there are over 900 facilities in the United States). But we would only ever expect to see **Postal Code** shown in separate attributes if the business needs to see it that way.

Check that repeating attributes are moved to a new entity.

Also as part of first normal form (1NF), when there are two or more of the same attribute in the same entity, they are called repeating attributes. Repeating attributes often take a sequence number as part of their name such as phone number in the example on the following page. We would need to break this out into a new entity.

On the following model we moved the four home phone numbers for the **Customer** into their own entity, **Customer Home Phone**.

SCHEME | 83

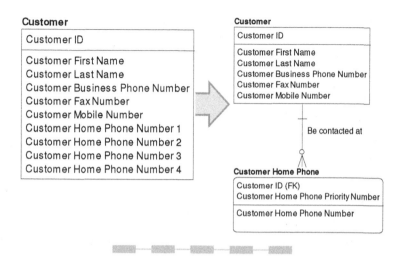

Check that every entity should have the minimal primary key.

For second normal form (2NF), each entity must have the minimal set of attributes that uniquely identify each entity instance. In the model below, **Employee's** primary key is **Employee Identifier** and **Department Code**. To put this entity into 2NF requires making sure we have the minimal primary key. We would have to confirm this, but the employee attributes most likely require only **Employee Identifier** and the department attributes require **Department Code**. We would also need to confirm the relationship between **Employee** and **Department**; in this model we learn that an **Employee** can work for more than one **Department**, and a **Department** can contain more than one **Employee**.

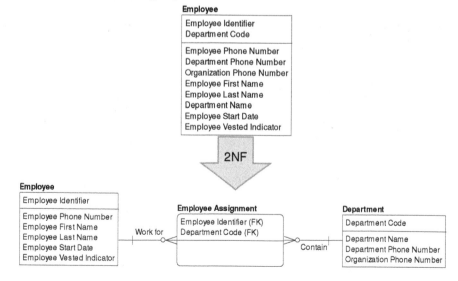

Make sure all hidden dependencies are removed.

Third normal form (3NF) requires the removal of hidden dependencies. A hidden dependency is when a property of an entity depends upon one or more other properties in that same entity instead of directly on that entity's primary key. Each attribute must be directly dependent on only the primary key and not directly dependent on any other attributes within the same entity. For example, assume an **Order** is identified by an **Order Number**. Within **Order**, there are many attributes including **Order Scheduled Delivery Date**, **Order Actual Delivery Date**, and **Order On Time Indicator**. **Order On Time Indicator** contains either a Yes or a No, providing a fact about whether the **Order Actual Delivery Date** is less than or equal to the **Order Scheduled Delivery Date**. **Order On Time Indicator**, therefore, provides a fact about **Order Actual Delivery Date** and **Order Scheduled Delivery Date**, not directly about **Order Number**. **Order On Time Indicator** has a hidden dependency that must be addressed to put the model into 3NF. This model shows that one solution to reaching 3NF is to remove the attribute **Order On Time Indicator,** which removes the hidden dependency:

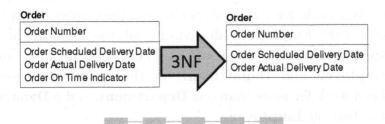

Make sure overlapping candidate keys are resolved.

Boyce Codd normal form (BCNF) states the model we are reviewing must not have overlapping candidate keys. Recall a candidate key is one or more attributes that uniquely identify a record. BCNF makes us check to make sure there are no business rules hiding between the primary and alternate keys. For example, assuming we are reviewing a data model containing this entity:

Enrollment

Course Number	
Student Number	
Course Name	(AK1:1)
Student Last Name	(AK1:2)
Enrollment Date	

SCHEME | 85

We have two candidate keys, the composite primary key on **Course Number** and **Student Number** and the composite alternate key on **Course Name** and **Student Last Name**. Are there any rules hiding between the keys? There is a good chance and we will have to confirm that the **Course Name** is identified by a **Course Number** and the **Student Last Name** is identified by a **Student Number**. **Enrollment Date** appears to require both **Course Number** and **Student Number,** so it is fine where it is. The model below is now in BCNF.

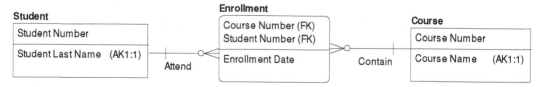

Note that **Student Last Name** is a very poor choice for an alternate key, but this example does illustrate how to ensure BCNF.

Make sure rules in complex primary keys are shown.

Higher levels of normalization such as fourth normal form (4NF), require showing the rules in complex primary keys. "Complex" usually means there are three or more identifying relationships. On the following model, there are three identifying relationships in **Employee Language Skill** and some complex rules hiding in this key as an **Employee** can speak **Languages** and an **Employee** can master **Skills**. Both of these rules need to be shown. See sample data and the resolved model on the next page.

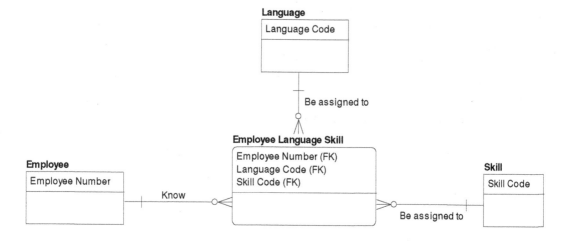

Employee	Skill	Language
Bob Smith	Data Modeling	English
Bob Smith	Data Modeling	Spanish
Bob Smith	Juggling	English
Bob Smith	Juggling	Spanish
Mary Jones	Proj Mgmt	English
Mary Jones	Proj Mgmt	French
Mary Jones	Proj Mgmt	German

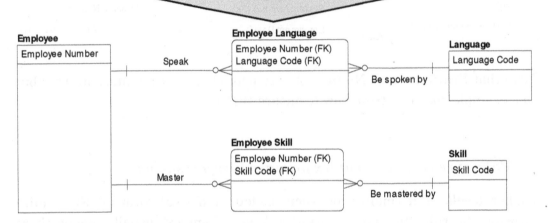

We realized that **Employee Language Skill** is hiding two relationships, one between **Employee** and **Language** and the second between **Employee** and **Skill**: an **Employee** may speak one or many **Languages**, and an **Employee** may master one or many **Skills**.

―――――――――

Check that each subtype's primary key is a foreign key to its supertype.

So for example on the following model, **Account Number** is the primary key of the supertype **Account**, and therefore also the primary keys for the subtypes **Savings Account** and **Checking Account**.

SCHEME | 87

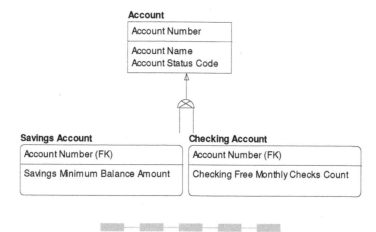

Dimensional Adherence

In addition to the general logical data model checks discussed previously, if the logical data model you are reviewing is dimensional, you will also need to apply the checks in this section.

> *Ensure the dimensional logical data model captured the solution, along with the navigation paths required to answer the business questions.*

As mentioned with the definition of a logical data model, we need to include everything that will meet the business requirements without complicating the structure with technology (which we will do in the physical). In addition, because the model we are reviewing is dimensional, we would expect the relationship lines to represent navigation paths.

> *Ensure that the model is fine-grained enough to answer the business questions around a business process.*

The grain is the lowest level of detail in the meter, the entity which contains the attributes that are being measured. We need to make sure the grain is at a level that can answer the required business questions. For example, if the following data model is being reviewed and the business question is "What is my daily **Account Balance Amount?**", we would have a problem because the lowest grain for calendar is **Month** and not **Date**.

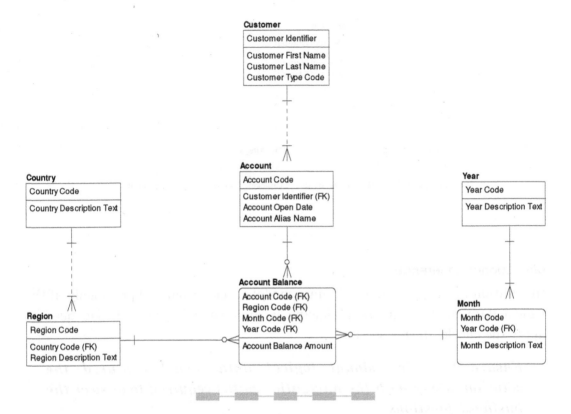

Make sure there is mandatory cardinality between the dimension levels.

All relationships between dimension levels must be mandatory. We need to avoid foreign key nulls on a dimensional model. If a specific **Product** does not roll up to a specific **Product Line,** for example, using a default value instead of leaving the foreign key in **Product** empty will minimize reporting errors.

On the following model, because there is mandatory cardinality on both sides of each of the relationships in this sales organization hierarchy, we cannot have empty nodes. If Bob at the **Region** level reports directly to the **National** level (skipping the **Zone** level), we need to put some value at the **Zone** level such as a 99 placeholder.

SCHEME | 89

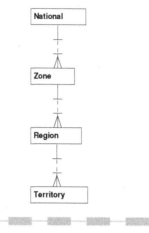

Make sure relationships don't cross dimensions.

Dimension levels should never have relationships to levels from other dimensions. This causes loops that lead to user and BI tool complexities by allowing for more than one way to navigate between the same structures. All relationships from dimensions must go through the meter. So for example, in the **Product** dimension there should not be a reference from the **Calendar** dimension capturing the year a product was first introduced into the market. This would cause a relationship between dimensions.

Before:

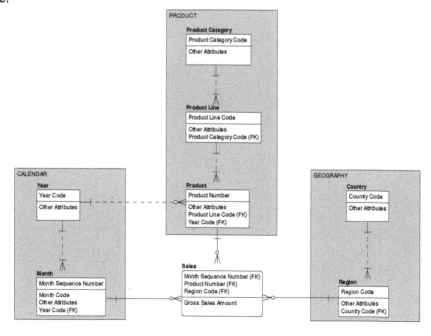

After:

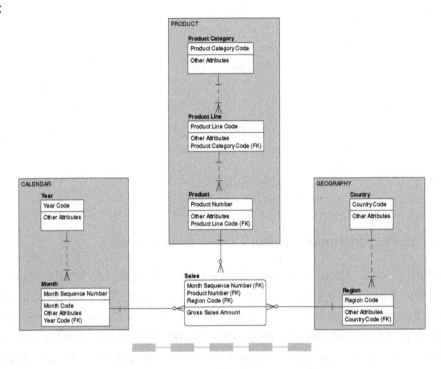

Ensure the model does not contain fuzzy grain.

Fuzzy grain is when there are relationships from different levels in the same dimension to the same meter. Here is an example of fuzzy grain:

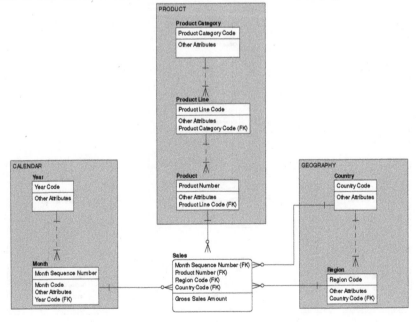

SCHEME | 91

This model has a relationship from **Country** to the meter that creates fuzzy grain because it is unclear as to the grain—is it at a **Region** or **Country** level? Here fuzzy grain is removed:

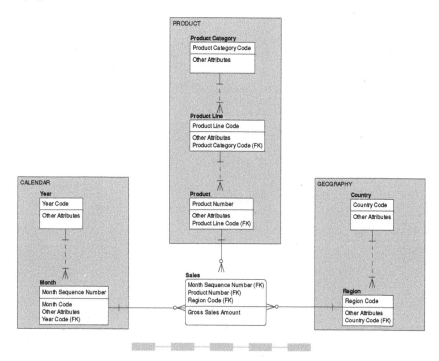

Check that the dimensional data model contains no subtypes.

Subtyping is a relational concept for grouping common properties together and is not useful for navigation and therefore an unnecessary complexity on the dimensional model.

Before:

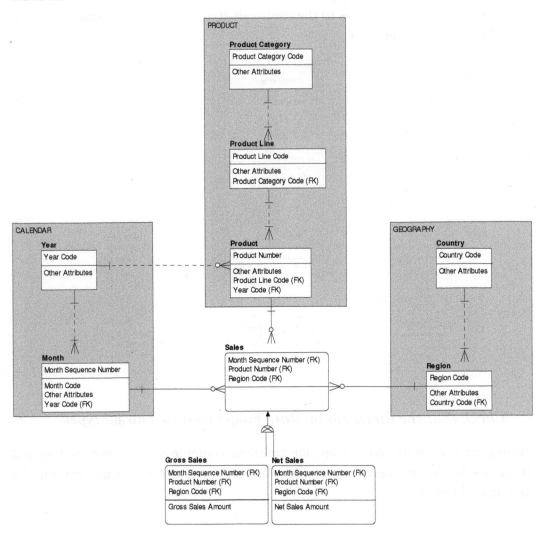

SCHEME | 93

After:

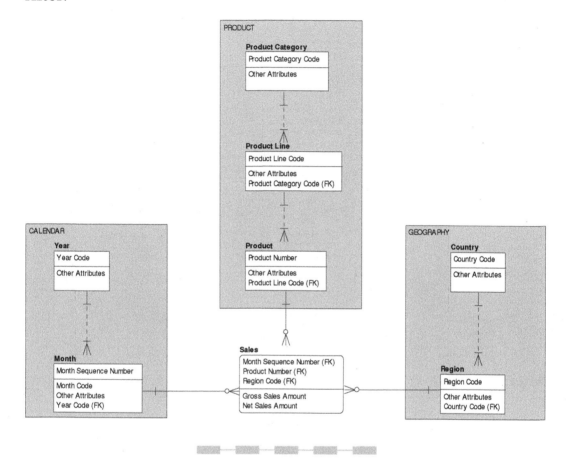

Check that the dimensional data model does not contain recursive relationships.

Recursive relationships are not simple and therefore should not be used on a dimensional model. Instead, the structure is frequently flattened by identifying the maximum number of levels possible in the recursive hierarchy or network structure.

Before:

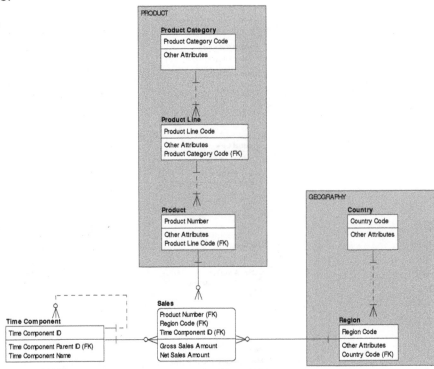

After:

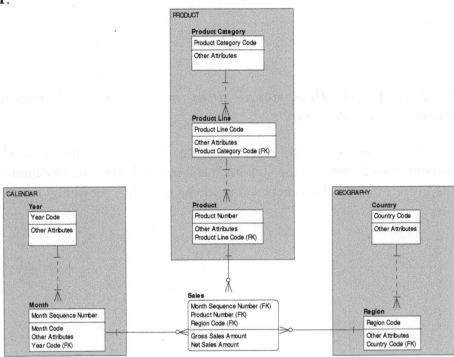

SCHEME | 95

Ensure conformed dimensions are created to integrate data across the enterprise.

Conformed dimensions are dimensions built with the organization perspective instead of a project prospective to support the ability to drill across and integrate data from multiple business processes. On the previous model, if **Calendar** is a conformed dimension, then this dimension can be used by multiple analytical applications.

PHYSICAL DATA MODEL ADHERENCE

All physical data models should follow the expectations in this section, plus the additional expectations in the relational or dimensional subsections depending on whether the model is a relational or dimensional data model.

Check that the physical data model captures the technical solution.

The physical data model contains all of the details needed to meet the business requirements, yet it also can be compromised for a given set of technology.

Check that non-unique indexes are used where necessary on a physical data model.

Non-unique indexes (also known as Inversion Entries) are added to improve retrieval performance and are therefore part of the technical solution. On the data model below, there are non-unique indexes on **Student Last Name** and **Student First Name**. We would need to confirm the requirements specify that sometimes **Student First Name** is being queried and sometimes **Student Last Name**.

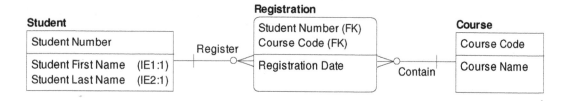

When natural keys are cumbersome or contain sensitive data, check that a physical data model uses a surrogate key.

When a natural primary key contains several attributes, it is advisable to create a single key that will be used as the physical primary key. This is referred to as a "surrogate" primary key because it substitutes for the natural key. The attributes that make up the natural candidate key should remain as attributes of the entity but be defined as an alternate key. Surrogate keys can also be added when the natural keys contain sensitive data that we would not want propagated to other structures through foreign keys. In the following example, we created the surrogate key **Student ID** and defined an alternate key on the combination of **Student Last Name**, **Student First Name**, and **Student Birth Date**, as well as defined a second alternate key on **Student Number**.

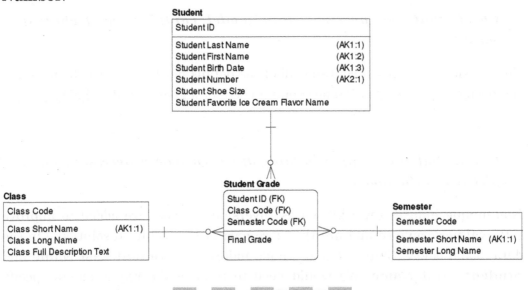

Check for proper use of audit attributes on a physical.

Audit attributes are used to document the status of a row in the database. Here are some common audit attributes:

Name	Definition
Created By User Identifier	The user identifier of the user that created the row in the table.
Created Datetime	The date/time that the row was created.

SCHEME | 97

Name	Definition
Last Updated By User Identifier	The user identifier of the user that last modified the row in the table.
Last Update Datetime	The date/time that the row was last updated.

Check that views were considered before denormalizing on a physical.

Denormalization is when structures are combined to improve performance or usability at the expense of added redundancy and reduced referential integrity (i.e., fewer relationships). For example, we can take these **Organization**, **Survey Creation**, and **Survey** logical normalized entities:

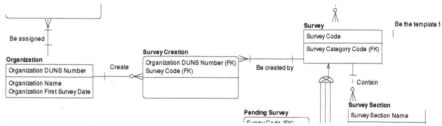

Organization

DUNS	Name	First Survey Dt
123	IBM	Apr 10 2014
789	Walmart	Sept 2 2013
566	Publyk House	Dec 23 2013

Survey Creation

DUNs	Survey Code
123	AB3
123	RE2
123	ZY6
789	ZY6
566	AB3
566	ZY6

Survey

Survey Code	Survey Category Code
AB3	CONSAT
RE2	EMPSAT
ZY6	MKTRSH

And denormalize them as shown on the following page. However, we can also build a view that looks identical to the denormalized structure above yet preserves the normalized perspective because the view is built upon the tables. The view provides a user-friendly structure, and depending on how it is implemented, it may have similar performance traits as the denormalized structure.

Survey Creation

Organization DUNs Number Survey Code
Survey Category Code Organization Name Organization First Survey Date

Survey Creation

DUNs	Survey Code	Survey Cat Code	Org Name	Org First Survey Dt
123	AB3	CONSAT	IBM	Apr 10 2014
123	RE2	EMPSAT	IBM	Apr 10 2014
123	ZY6	MKTRSH	IBM	Apr 10 2014
789	ZY6	MKTRSH	Walmart	Sept 2 2013
566	AB3	CONSAT	Publyk House	Dec 23 2013
566	ZY6	MKTRSH	Publyk House	Dec 23 2013

Views are great because an underlying normalized structure can be preserved while the views present the more user-friendly structure. Also, data can be stored one place in the underlying structures yet presented many different ways through views. Just beware of the possible difficulties of inserting or updating through a view.

Relational Adherence

In addition to the general physical data model checks discussed previously, if the physical data model you are reviewing is relational, you will also need to apply the checks in this section.

Ensure the relational physical data model captures the technical solution along with the business rules that exist between the structures.

The physical data model contains all of the details needed to meet the business requirements, yet it is also compromised for a given set of technology. Because the model is relational, our focus is on communicating and enforcing business rules. Therefore, in a relational database the relationship lines represent database constraints.

SCHEME | 99

Check that there are no subtypes on the physical.

The subtyping symbol cannot exist on a physical data model (unless the model we are building is for an object-oriented database), so expect subtyping to be resolved one of three ways: Identity, Rolldown, and Rollup:

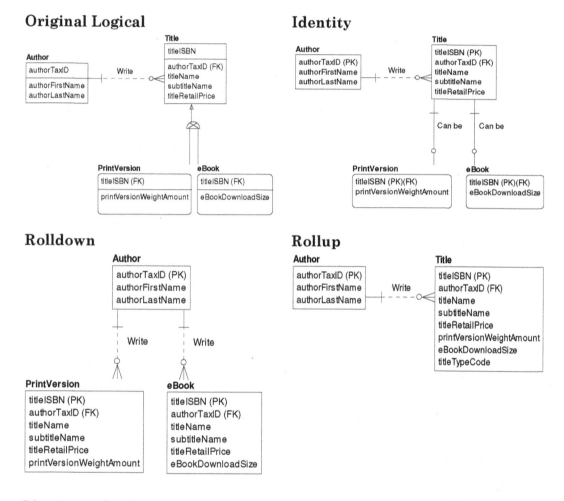

Identity is the closest to subtyping because the subtyping symbol is replaced with a one-to-one relationship for each supertype/subtype combination. The main advantage of identity is that all of the business rules at the supertype level and at the subtype level remain the same as in the logical data model. That is, we can continue to enforce relationships at the supertype or subtype levels as well as enforce that certain fields be required at the supertype or subtype levels. Identity allows us to still require the **eBookDownloadSize** for **eBook**, for example. The main disadvantage of identity is that it can take more time to retrieve data as it requires navigating multiple tables to access both the supertype and subtype information.

Rolldown means we are moving the attributes and relationships of the supertype down to each of the subtypes. Rolling down can produce a more user-friendly structure than identity or rolling up because subtypes are often more concrete concepts than supertypes, making it easier for the users of the data model to relate to the subtypes. However, we are repeating relationships and attributes, which could reduce any user-friendliness gained from removing the supertype. In addition, the rolling down technique may lead to not enforcing the rules at the supertype. This could lead to a less flexible data model as we can no longer easily accommodate new subtypes without modifying the data model. If a new type of **Title** is required in addition to **PrintVersion** and **eBook**, this would require effort to accommodate. Also, querying all **Titles** requires searching both tables

Rollup means rolling up the subtypes up into the supertype. The subtypes disappear, and all attributes and relationships only exist at the supertype level. Rolling up adds flexibility to the data model because new types of the supertype can be added, often with no model changes. However, rolling up can also produce a more obscure model as the audience for the model may not relate to the supertype as well as they would to the subtypes. When we roll up, we often need a way to distinguish the original subtypes from each other, so we frequently add a type column such as **titleTypeCode**. Without this type column, it becomes more difficult to enforce rules that were easy to enforce at the subtype level—for example, ensuring **eBookDownloadSize** is mandatory for **eBooks**.

Dimensional Adherence

In addition to the general physical data model checks discussed previously, if the physical data model you are reviewing is dimensional, you will also need to apply the checks in this section.

> *Ensure the dimensional physical data model captures the technical solution along with the navigation paths required to answer the business questions.*

The physical data model contains all of the details needed to meet the business requirements, yet it is also can be compromised for a given set of technology.

SCHEME | 101

Because the model is dimensional, our focus is on designing navigation paths, making it simple, secure, and speedy to return the answers to business questions.

Ensure proper use of summarizations on a dimensional physical.

If significant retrieval performance benefits can be shown, summarizations are a very effective design technique. For example, on the data model below, the modeler has decided to summarize sales up to a day, month, and year.

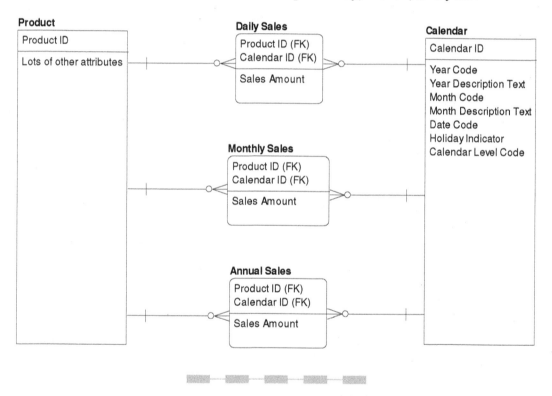

Ensure proper use of junk dimensions on a dimensional physical.

A junk dimension is a dimension containing all the possible combinations of a small and somewhat related set of indicators and codes. It is most useful when two or more dimensions contain a relatively low number of records, are somewhat related, and are used often together in queries. In the example below, the **Gender**, **Shoe Size**, and **Height Range** dimensions have been combined into a single **Employee Characteristic** dimension.

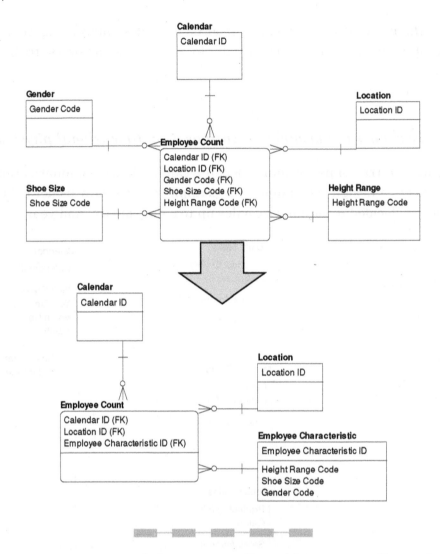

Ensure proper use of degenerate dimensions on a dimensional physical.

A degenerate dimension is a dimension whose attribute(s) have been moved to the fact table. The meter on a dimensional logical data model becomes one or more fact tables on the dimensional physical data model. A degenerate dimension is most common when the original dimension contained only a single attribute such as a transaction identifier. In the following example, the **Order** dimension just contains a single attribute, the **Order Number**, and therefore we can remove the **Order** dimension and keep the **Order Number** as a foreign key in the fact table.

SCHEME | 103

Before:

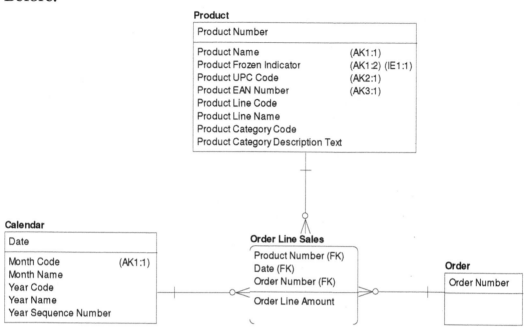

After:

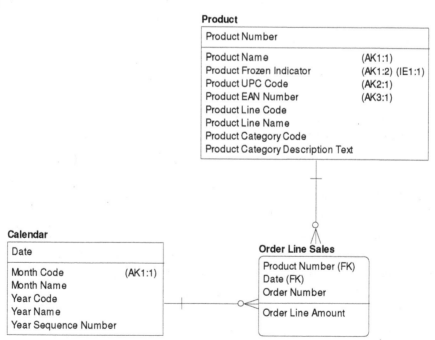

Avoid recommending a degenerate dimension if the attribute has values that are frequently selected. For example, on the following model, **Gender** has been made a degenerate dimension. Imagine, however, that a user is requesting a particular **Gender** (male or female) from a drop-down menu, and instead of the choices Male and Female returning in a sub second response time, a select distinct is being run against the fact table which contains millions of records, therefore taking a lot longer time to return!

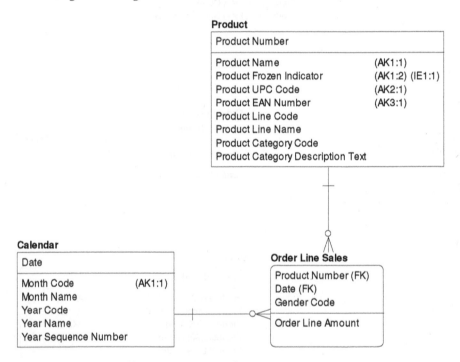

NoSQL Database Adherence

There are currently four main types of NoSQL databases:

- **Document databases** are query friendly and very intuitive. It is easy to visualize much of what an organization does on a daily basis in terms of documents. A customer places an order, so there is a **Purchase Order** document. An organization bills a customer, so there is an **Invoice** document. Someone is searching for a book in the library, so there is a **Card Catalog** document.

- **Column databases** store similar types of data together, and therefore these types of databases are excellent at compression and retrieval performance. For example, if all of the **Gross Sales Amounts** are

SCHEME | 105

stored together, analyzing **Gross Sales Amount** will take much less time than if **Gross Sales Amount** is stored with each **Order**. If certain instances are missing attributes or have additional attributes, column easily accommodates. Also, by storing like data types together, compression can be applied, saving space and increasing retrieval performance.

- **Key-value databases** are the most simplistic in structure, where essentially any data can be stored along with an identifier to retrieve this data. Key-value is also great for versioning, and because of its simple structure and commands (put, get, and delete), it is ideal for extremely high volumes of small important transactions. For example, Amazon created the key-value database Dynamo to manage its consumer shopping carts.

- **Graph databases** are used when relationships are more important than attributes as in social media and optimization efforts like the Traveling Salesperson problem. Often these situations involve open-linked data where there can be any number of "things" related to any other number of "things."

Each of these types of databases requires a set of design best practices, and then there are specific products within each type of database that have more refined best practices. For example, there could be something that works well in MongoDB but not MarkLogic even though both products are document-based databases.

If you are reviewing a physical data model for a NoSQL database, become familiar with the design best practices for your particular product. Then document these best practices so others can leverage them too.

Summary of Scheme Checks

Conceptual (general):
- ✓ Confirm the conceptual data model captures the business needs and scope of the application.
- ✓ Confirm all entities on a conceptual are basic and critical to the audience.
- ✓ Catch any attributes on the conceptual, unless the attributes themselves are basic and critical to the audience.
- ✓ Make sure many-to-many relationships have not been resolved on a conceptual unless the resolving entity is itself basic and critical to the project.

Conceptual (relational):
- ✓ Ensure the relational conceptual data model captures the business needs and scope of the application along with the business rules that exist between the conceptual entities.
- ✓ Ensure each relationship captures the answer to four business questions.
- ✓ Make sure every subtype has one and only one supertype.
- ✓ Make sure relational modeling is used when needing adhoc reporting.

Conceptual (dimensional):
- ✓ Ensure the dimensional conceptual data model captures the business needs and scope of the application along with the navigation paths required to answer the business questions.
- ✓ Make sure a dimensional model is built when there is a requirement to analyze measures.
- ✓ Challenge a dimensional model that is more fine-grained than necessary.

Logical (general):
- ✓ Ensure the logical data model captures the business solution.
- ✓ Make sure all candidate keys are unique, stable, and mandatory (not null).
- ✓ Check that many-to-many relationships are resolved on a logical data model.
- ✓ Make sure there are no non-unique indexes on a logical data model.
- ✓ Ensure surrogate keys only appear on a logical data model when new concepts are introduced.
- ✓ Make sure every entity contains a primary key.
- ✓ Make sure every relationship has a corresponding foreign key.

SCHEME | 107

Summary of Scheme Checks (continued)

Logical (relational):
- ✓ Ensure the relational logical data model captured the business solution, along with the business rules that exist between the logical entities.
- ✓ Check that multi-valued attributes are separated.
- ✓ Check that repeating attributes are moved to a new entity.
- ✓ Check that every entity should have the minimal primary key.
- ✓ Make sure all hidden dependencies are removed.
- ✓ Make sure overlapping candidate keys are resolved.
- ✓ Make sure rules in complex primary keys are shown.
- ✓ Check that each subtype's primary key is a foreign key to its supertype.

Logical (dimensional):
- ✓ Ensure the dimensional logical data model captured the solution, along with the navigation paths required to answer the business questions.
- ✓ Ensure that the model is fine-grained enough to answer the business questions around a business process.
- ✓ Make sure there is mandatory cardinality between the dimension levels.
- ✓ Make sure relationships don't cross dimensions.
- ✓ Ensure the model does not contain fuzzy grain.
- ✓ Check that the dimensional data model contains no subtypes.
- ✓ Check that the dimensional data model does not contain recursive relationships.
- ✓ Ensure conformed dimensions are created to integrate data across the enterprise.

Physical (general):
- ✓ Check that the physical data model captures the technical solution.
- ✓ Check that non-unique indexes are used where necessary on a physical data model.
- ✓ When natural keys are cumbersome or contain sensitive data, check that a physical data model uses a surrogate key.
- ✓ Check for proper use of audit attributes on a physical.
- ✓ Check that views were considered before denormalizing on a physical.

Summary of Scheme Checks (continued)

Physical (relational):
- ✓ Ensure the relational physical data model captures the technical solution along with the business rules that exist between the structures.
- ✓ Check that there are no subtypes on the physical.

Physical (dimensional):
- ✓ Ensure the dimensional physical data model captures the technical solution along with the navigation paths required to answer the business questions.
- ✓ Ensure proper use of summarizations on a dimensional physical.
- ✓ Ensure proper use of junk dimensions on a dimensional physical.
- ✓ Ensure proper use of degenerate dimensions on a dimensional physical.

Physical (NoSQL):
- ✓ If you are reviewing a physical data model for a NoSQL database, become familiar with the design best practices for your particular product. Then document these best practices so others can leverage them too.

Chapter 7
Category Four: Structure
How structurally sound is the model?

The "Structure" category validates the design practices employed to build the model. Assume you were comfortable reading an architectural blueprint and somebody shared their house blueprint with you. If there was a garage drawn in the attic, you would catch it. You would notice that something just does not seem right on the blueprint. The blueprint is to a house as the data model is to a database. Therefore, if there was something not quite right on the data model, you would catch it as well. Many of these structure issues are quickly and automatically flagged by our modeling and database tools. Examples include prohibiting having two attributes with the same exact name in the same entity, a null attribute in a primary key, and most types of circular relationships.

CATEGORY EXPECTATIONS

This section contains a subset of what to look for to grade the Structure category. There are three categories of structural soundness issues: *Consistency*, *Integrity*, and *Core*. Consistency means that if there are two or more of the same attribute on the data model, everything about these duplicated attributes is consistent such as formatting, lengths, and definitions. Integrity means a database structure can be generated successfully from the data model. Core means that the basic rules of data modeling are being followed.

MODEL IS CONSISTENT

As stated above, consistency means that if there are two or more of the same attribute on the data model, everything about these duplicated attributes is consistent such as formatting, lengths, and definitions.

Check that if an attribute appears more than once in the same data model, it has the same definition for each occurrence.

In the example below, the attribute **Price** appears in the **Menu** entity and also in the **Order_Line** entity, but it has a different definition depending on where it appears. We need to recommend renaming the attributes, as we did in this example.

Before	After
Menu.Price: This is the retail amount of an item offered for purchase in our restaurant.	Menu.Retail_Price: This is the retail amount of an item offered for purchase in our restaurant.
Order_Line.Price: This is the actual amount of an item in our restaurant. For example, the restaurant manager might have adjusted the price in reaction to a customer complaint.	Order_Line.Actual_Price: This is the actual amount of an item in our restaurant. For example, the restaurant manager might have adjusted the price in reaction to a customer complaint.

Check that the same definition is not used for two different attributes.

In the example below, we needed to distinguish the definitions to reflect two distinct attributes, **Retail_Price** and **Actual_Price**.

Before	After
Menu.Retail_Price: This is the retail amount of an item offered for purchase in our restaurant.	Menu.Retail_Price: This is the retail amount of an item offered for purchase in our restaurant.
Order_Line.Actual_Price: This is the retail amount of an item offered for purchase in our restaurant.	Order_Line.Actual_Price: This is the actual amount of an item in our restaurant. For example, the restaurant manager might have adjusted the price in reaction to a customer complaint.

Check that if an attribute appears more than once in the same data model, it has the same format, datatype, and other details for each occurrence.

In the model below, **Account Number** is nine characters in the **Account** supertype and **Checking Account** subtype entities, yet only seven characters in the **Savings Account** entity.

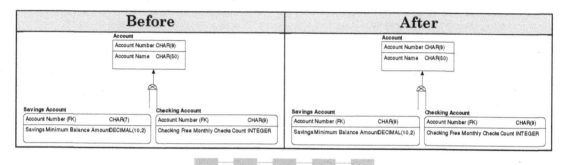

Avoid classword mismatches.

In the example below, the book's subtitle is a date format. A Name classword should not have a Date format. We also need to fix the Integer format for **Title Name** and the Character format for **Publication Date**.

Before	After
Title	**Title**
Title Name — INTEGER	Title Name — CHAR(50)
Subtitle Name — DATE Publication Date CHAR(50)	Subtitle Name — CHAR(75) Publication Date DATE

MODEL HAS INTEGRITY

Integrity means a database structure can be generated from the data model.

Ensure that there are no circular relationships.

A circular relationship is when no entity instances can be created because in order to create an entity instance, we first need to create an entity instance of another entity, which depends on the original entity. So we are caught in a "catch-22" where no entity instances can be created. In the model below, we cannot create a **Customer** instance until we create their **Account Primary Number**. However, in order to create the **Account** for **Account Primary**

Number, we first need to create the **Customer ID**, causing an infinite loop. Therefore, no entity instances can be created. I recommend making one of the relationships optional, as done in this example.

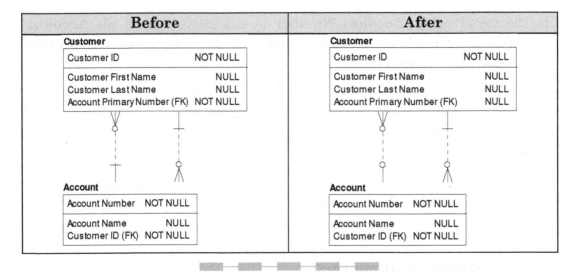

Check that a mandatory relationship is associated with a not null foreign key.

In the model below, the **Class Code** foreign key is defined as NULL in **Student Grade**, yet the cardinality on the relationship back to **Class** indicates that **Class Code** must be mandatory instead of optional. Note that we would expect **Class Code** to be a required attribute because it is part of **Student Grade's** primary key. So we would need to make the foreign key **Class Code** NOT NULL instead of NULL.

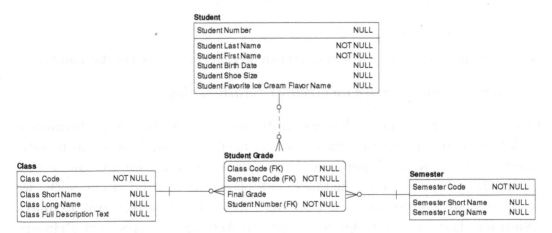

Check that an optional relationship is associated with a null foreign key.

On the data model above, **Student Number** is a NOT NULL foreign key, yet the cardinality on the relationship back to **Student** is optional, meaning that the **Student Number** foreign key should be NULL instead of NOT NULL.

Check that all attributes in each candidate key are NOT NULL.

Each attribute in a primary or alternate key must be required and NOT NULL. On the following model, **ISBN** is an alternate key, yet it is defined as NULL. Either we need to make it mandatory (NOT NULL) or remove the alternate key.

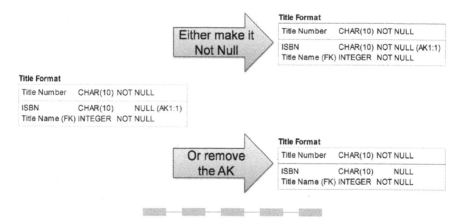

Catch any attributes appearing more than once in the same entity.

In **Account**, the **Account Name** attribute seems to appear twice. One of these occurrences should be removed unless it has a different meaning, in which case it should be renamed.

Before	After
Account	**Account**
Account Number	Account Number
AccountName Account Name	Account Name

Catch any entities appearing more than once on the same model.

On this model, **Customer** appears three times. It should only appear once.

Before	After
Customer customer CUSTOMER	Customer

Make sure each entity has a primary key.

On the model below, the supertype **Account** is missing its primary key, and therefore the subtypes are also missing this primary key. To fix this issue, we will need to add a primary key to **Account**; then this primary key will be inherited to both of the subtypes.

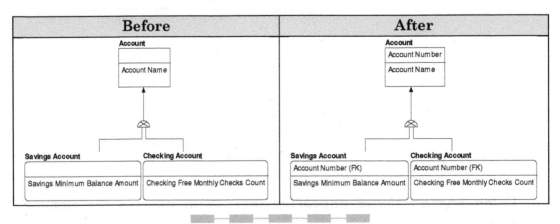

Make sure there are no reserved words as attribute names.

The attribute **Table** in the **Office** entity below should be renamed to **Office Table Quantity** so that the reserved word "table" is not used.

Before	After
Office Office Location Code Office Window Quantity Table	**Office** Office Location Code Office Window Quantity Office Table Quantity

MODEL FOLLOWS CORE PRINCIPLES

Core means that the basic rules of data modeling are being followed.

Make sure each entity has a relationship with at least one other entity in the model.

In the following model, there is no relationship between **Account Type** and **Account**, yet **Account** does have the foreign key **Account Type Code**. To fix this problem, we will need to add the missing relationship. Note that there are valid cases where an entity may not have any relationships such as in the case of generic lookup entities. However, we need to challenge the standalone entities to make sure there are valid reasons why these entities have no relationships.

Before	After
Account Type Account Type Code Account Type Name **Account** Account Number Account Type Code Account Name	**Account Type** Account Type Code Account Type Name **Account** Account Number Account Type Code (FK) Account Name

Catch all partial key relationships.

A foreign key is an attribute that provides a link to another entity. When a relationship is created between two entities, the entity on the "many" side of the relationship contains the primary key from the entity on the "one" side of the relationship. If only part of the primary key is copied cover, this is called a partial key relationship. A partial key relationship is a relationship between two entities, yet the primary key from the parent entity is not completely propagated to the child entity.

In the following example, **Region Code** should also appear in the **Employee** entity and be part of the foreign key.

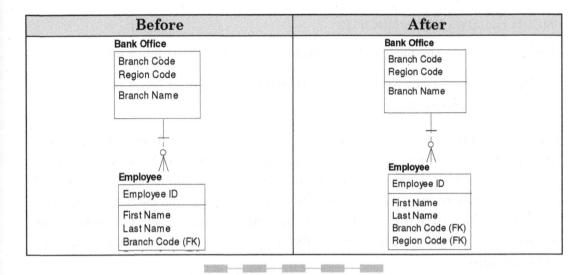

Catch when there are two relationships but only one foreign key.

This could mean that one of the relationships is unnecessary, or it could mean that both relationships represent important rules and a foreign key from one of them is missing, in which case we will need the *role name* to have both foreign keys in the same entity. Role naming is when we rename a foreign key with a different name than its primary key.

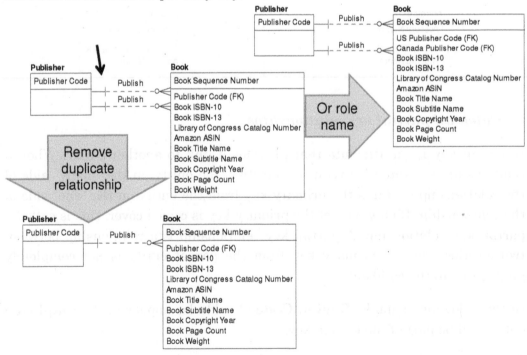

In the previous data model, there are two relationships from **Publisher** to **Book** but only one foreign key, **Publisher Code**. We can either remove the duplicate relationship, or we can role name the foreign key, so that each foreign key has a different name (**US Publisher Code** and **Canada Publisher Code**).

Catch redundant indexes.

For example, a primary key that is just a single attribute does not require a separate non-unique index. In **Account** below, **Account Number** is the primary key so it is automatically indexed by default, yet there is an extra index added (IE 1.1) that offers no value. "IE" stands for "Inversion Entry," and it means a secondary non-unique index added to improve retrieval performance. We would need to remove this secondary index.

Before	After
Account Account Number (IE1:1) Account Name	**Account** Account Number Account Name

Make sure subtypes have the same primary key as their supertype.

In the example below, **Checking Account** has a different primary key than **Account**. Subtypes are examples of supertypes, and therefore a subtype must have the same primary key as the supertype. **Savings Account** has **Account Number** as its primary key, as does **Account**, but **Checking Account** also has **Checking Account Sequence Number** as part of its key. We need to make the primary key of **Checking Account** just the **Account Number**.

Before	After

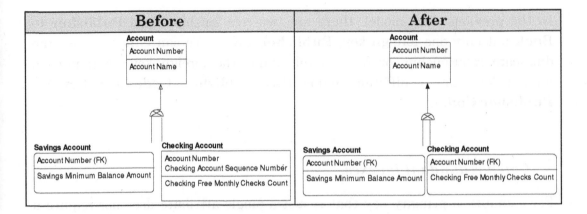

Summary of Structure Checks

Consistency:
✓ Check that if an attribute appears more than once in the same data model, it has the same definition for each occurrence.
✓ Check that the same definition is not used for two different attributes.
✓ Check that if an attribute appears more than once in the same data model, it has the same format, datatype, and other details for each occurrence.
✓ Avoid classword mismatches.

Integrity:
✓ Ensure that there are no circular relationships.
✓ Check that a mandatory relationship is associated with a not null foreign key.
✓ Check that an optional relationship is associated with a null foreign key.
✓ Check that all attributes in each candidate key are NOT NULL.
✓ Catch any attributes appearing more than once in the same entity.
✓ Catch any entities appearing more than once on the same model.
✓ Make sure each entity has a primary key.
✓ Make sure there are no reserved words as attribute names.

Core:
✓ Make sure each entity has a relationship with at least one other entity in the model.
✓ Catch all partial key relationships.
✓ Catch when there are two relationships but only one foreign key.
✓ Catch redundant indexes.
✓ Make sure subtypes have the same primary key as their supertype.

Chapter 8
Category Five: Abstraction
How well does the model leverage generic structures?

The "Abstraction" category confirms a proper balance on the model between flexibility and usability. One of the most powerful tools a data modeler has at their disposal is abstraction, the ability to increase the types of information a design can accommodate using generic concepts. Going from concepts such as **Customer** and **Employee** to **Person** and **Person Role,** for example, increases flexibility but also reduces the use of the data model as a communication tool.

I visualize the abstraction setting as a volume control, where the greater the volume, the greater the use of abstraction.

The higher the volume, the closer we get to these six concepts:

- **Who?** Who is important to the business?
- **What?** What does the business do?
- **When?** When is business conducted?
- **Where?** Where is business conducted?
- **Why?** Why is the business in business?
- **How?** How do we document events?

For example, if we blast the "Who" setting, we may have the entity **Party**. If we turn down the power slightly, we may have entities **Person** and **Organization**. If we turn down the volume further, we may have **Employee**. Turning it down further would lead to **Full Time Employee** and **Part Time Employee**.

If we blast the "What" setting, we have a very generic structure for **Product** or **Service**; for example, in the publishing industry I know of a publisher who uses **Intellectual Unit** to represent many products including books. Turning down the power slightly, we may have **Product** or **Service,** and turning down the power further we may have **Book,** and then even further **Print Book** and **Electronic Book**.

If we blast the "When" setting, we have a very generic view of time such as **Time Component**. Turning down the power leads to concepts such as **Month** and **Year**. If we blast the "Where" setting, we have **Location Component,** and turning down the volume all of the way we have **Postal Code** or **Website**. If we blast the "Why" setting, we have an **Event** or **Transaction**. Turning down the power, we have an **Order**, **Credit**, or **Trade**.

If we blast the "How" setting, we have **Document**. Turning down the power slightly we have **Agreement** and **Contract**, and turning down the power all the way we have **Purchase Order** or **Invoice**. "How" captures how events get recorded. How is similar to the paper trail, where the event **Order** for example, will have the document **Purchase Order** recording that this event occurred.

CATEGORY EXPECTATIONS

This section contains a subset of what to look for to grade the Abstraction category. For each data model that is reviewed, knowing which is valued more, flexibility or usability, helps us gauge the amount of abstraction that should appear on the model.

MODEL IS EXTENSIBLE

This section contains the expectations for increasing the level of abstraction on the model.

>   ***Expect to see abstraction if flexibility is valued more than usability.***

We would expect to see the abstract **Party Role** model below if flexibility is valued more than usability. A **Party** can be a person or organization, and that person or organization can play many roles. One of these roles is **Customer**.

Not abstract	Abstract
Customer	Party ⊢── Play ──< Party Role

Recommend a supertype when there is optionality on both ends of relationships.

Introducing the **Offering** supertype on the model below fixes the two relationships with optionality on both sides.

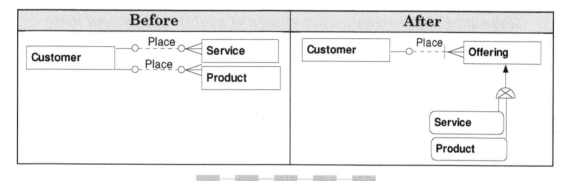

Before	After

Suggest abstracting similar types of concepts if there are valid business scenarios where future types of this same concept can occur.

In the model below there are lots of phone numbers, so the chance of an additional type of phone number occurring is high. Therefore this could be a candidate for abstraction, and we would abstract as shown below.

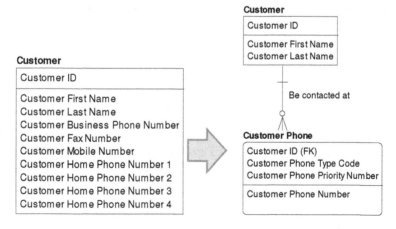

We can replace all of these phone numbers with just the **Customer Phone** structure. **Customer Phone Type Code** can have values such as 01 for Fax and 02 for Mobile. The **Customer Phone Priority Number** allows for multiple fax numbers, for example, and assigns an importance so we can try a certain fax number first. **Customer Phone Number** contains the actual phone number such as 212-555-1212.

MODEL IS USEABLE

This section contains the expectations for decreasing the level of abstraction on the model.

Make sure abstraction wasn't chosen if usability is valued more than flexibility.

In our previous example with **Customer** and **Party**, we would choose to use **Customer** if usability is valued more than flexibility. Note we need not abstract in reporting applications where simplicity and speed are paramount.

Make sure abstraction wasn't chosen to reduce or eliminate business conversations.

For example, if there are lots of debates as to what a customer is, the modeler may be tempted to remove **Customer** from the model entirely to save time and just replace it with the generic **Party** and **Party Role** concepts. But abstracting to avoid business conversations is not often productive as the issue is just being postponed—usually with an innocent developer paying the price (as well as the business).

Avoid ambiguous terms.

There are certain terms that just by their name have more than one definition depending on what part of the business is involved. On the model below, for example, because the primary key of **Product** is **Model Number**, we would be better off calling the entity **Model** instead of **Product**. **Product** can be very ambiguous—for example, the manufacturing section of the business might treat raw materials as products and the sales department might treat finished goods as products.

Before	After
Product Model Number Model Name	**Model** Model Number Model Name

---

Summary of Abstraction Checks

Extensible:
- ✓ Expect to see abstraction if flexibility is valued more than usability.
- ✓ Recommend a supertype when there is optionality on both ends of relationships.
- ✓ Suggest abstracting similar types of concepts if there are valid business scenarios where future types of this same concept can occur.

Useable:
- ✓ Make sure abstraction wasn't chosen if usability is valued more than flexibility.
- ✓ Make sure abstraction wasn't chosen to reduce or eliminate business conversations.
- ✓ Avoid ambiguous terms.

Chapter 9

Category Six: Standards

How well does the model follow naming standards?

The "Standards" category makes sure the data model adheres to naming standards including structure, term, and style.

Structure means that the proper building blocks are being used for entities, relationships, and attributes. For example, entities should be singular nouns, relationships should be present tense verbs, and attributes are traditionally built from three components: a subject (also known as a "prime"); zero, one, or more modifiers; and a classword (classwords are the last part of an attribute name such as "Name," "Code," or "Amount").

Term means that the proper name is given to the attribute or entity. Term includes proper spelling and abbreviation. An abbreviations list can be used to name each logical and physical term. Organizations should have a process in place for efficiently creating new abbreviations if a term cannot be found on a list.

Style means that the appearance, such as upper case or camelback case, is consistent with standard practices. Style includes whether the term should be plural or singular, whether hyphens, spaces, or camelback (initial upper case with no spaces in between words such as **customerLastName**) should be used, and case (i.e., upper case, initial upper case, or lower case).

The models in this book were created using ER/Studio. ER/Studio provides the capability to assign and import naming standards, making it easier to implement and update your naming standards.

CATEGORY EXPECTATIONS

This section contains a subset of what to look for to grade the Standards category.

MODEL IS WELL-STRUCTURED

Check that all entities are singular nouns.

Customer is singular and therefore acceptable, but **Customers** is plural and not advised, for example.

━━ ━━ ━━ ━━ ━━

Check that all relationships are present tense verbs.

"Each **Customer** must placing one or many **Offerings**" does not read as well as "Each **Customer** must place one or many **Offerings**":

Before	After
Customer —o- - Placing - -|< Offering	Customer —o- - Place - -|< Offering

━━ ━━ ━━ ━━ ━━

Check that all attributes include a prime; zero, one, or more modifiers; and a classword.

A prime is the subject the attribute describes, measures, or identifies such as **Customer**, **Product**, or **Sales**. Modifiers are terms that clarify the attribute such as "First" in **Customer First Name**. A classword is the last part of an attribute name that represents the high level domain in which the attribute belongs. Here are examples of the major classwords along with a brief description:

- Name. A textual value by which a thing, person, or concept is known. Examples: **Company Name**, **Customer Last Name**, **Product Name**
- Text. An unconstrained string of characters or any freeform comment or notes field. Examples: **Email Body Text**, **Tweet Text**, **Order Comments Text**
- Amount. A numeric measurement of monetary value in a particular currency such as dollars or Euros. Examples: **Order Total Amount**, **Employee Salary Amount**, **Product Retail Price Amount**
- Date. A calendar date. Examples: **Order Entry Date**, **Consumer Birth Date**, **Course Start Date**
- Code. A shortened form representing a descriptive piece of business information. Often a code will be a key to a reference table containing a

mostly fixed list. Examples: **Company Code**, **Employee Gender Code**, **Currency Code**

- Quantity. A measure of something in units. Quantity is a broad category containing any property that can be mathematically manipulated with the exception of currencies, which are Amounts. Quantity includes counts, weights, volumes, etc. Examples: **Order Quantity**, **Elevator Maximum Gross Weight**, **Claim Count**

- Number. Number can be misleading as it is usually a business key (that is, a business user's way of identifying a concept). Number cannot be mathematically manipulated and often contains letters and special characters such as the hyphen in the case of a telephone number. Examples: **Social Security Number**, **Credit Card Number**, **Employee Access Number**

- Identifier. A mandatory, stable, and unique property of an entity that is used to identify instances of that entity. Examples: **Case Identifier**, **Transaction Identifier**, **Product Identifier**

- Indicator. When there are only two values such as Yes or No, 1 or 0, True or False, On or Off. Sometimes called a "flag." Examples: **Student Graduation Indicator**, **Order Taxable Indicator**, **Current Record Indicator**

- Rate. A fraction indicating a proportion between two dissimilar things. Examples: **Employee Hourly Rate**, **State Tax Rate**, **Unemployment Rate**

- Percent. A ratio where 100 is understood as the denominator. Examples: **Ownership Percent**, **Gross Sales Change Percent**, **Net Return Percent**

- Complex. Anything that is not one of the above categories. This can include music, video, photographs, scanned images, documents, etc. Examples: **Employee Photo JPEG**, **Contract Signed PDF**, **Employee Phone Conversation MPP**

Catch relationship labels on a dimensional data model.

The relationships on a dimensional data model capture navigation paths and not business rules. Therefore, relationship labels are not needed on a dimensional data model.

Make sure the model does not exceed database-specific character limits.

Many databases limit how long a structure's name can be, so make sure you stick within their guidelines. If an attribute name cannot exceed 32 characters, for example, all attribute names need to be 32 characters or less.

Make sure rolenames have the same prime and classword as their primary key.

In the following example, the foreign key rolenames have the same prime "Publisher" and same classword "Code." They only differ in their modifiers ("US" and "Canada").

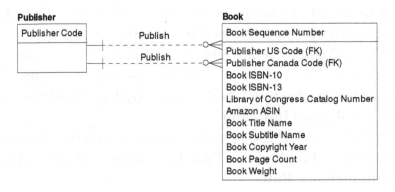

Check that attribute names are singular.

Before	After
Account Deposit Amounts	Account Deposit Amount

Check that the name of each foreign key attribute matches the primary key unless role naming is being used.

In this example, the foreign keys in **Customer Account** and **Account Balance** have the same names as their primary key counterparts.

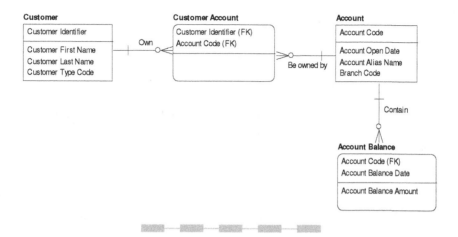

Ensure all attributes contain at most five modifiers.

Modifiers are listed after the prime and before the classword. Some attribute names do not require modifiers such as identifiers.

Too many modifiers	Acceptable
Order The Date That It Was Placed Date	Order Placement Date

Make sure entity names do not end with a classword.

An entity named **Customer Type Code**, for example, should be renamed to **Customer Type**.

Make sure the model avoids abbreviations and initialisms unless everyone knows what they mean.

Unknown Initialism	Fully-spelled out
LOB Code	Line of Business Code

Catch any prepositions (e.g., at, by, for, from, in, of, to), articles (e.g., a, an, the), and conjunctions (e.g., and, or, but) used in any name.

In the spirit of keeping names concise yet descriptive, avoid phrasing names in sentence format.

Sentence format	Acceptable
The First Name Of The Customer	Customer First Name

MODEL USES THE CORRECT TERMS

Check that a suffix of "Dimension" or "Fact" is used for all entities on a dimensional data model.

In dimensional modeling, it is a recommended practice to suffix dimension names with "Dimension," such as **Customer Dimension**, and suffix fact tables with "Fact" such as **Sales Fact**.

Make sure each relationship label captures the business reason for the relationship.

This quote from *Data and Reality* by William Kent summarizes the importance of the relationship label: *A relationship is an association among several things, with that association having a particular significance. For brevity, I will refer to the significance of an association as its 'reason'. There is an association between you and your car, for the reason that you own it. There's an association between a teacher and a class, because he teaches it. There's an association between a part and a warehouse, because the part is stored there.* Always think about what the reason is on the relationship line, and you will avoid label names such as *has, have, associate,* and *relate to.*

Bad	Good
Each **Machine** may be *associated with* one or many **Parts**.	Each **Machine** may *contain* one or many **Parts**.

Make sure each relationship has a pre-approved relationship label.

Come up with a predefined list of relationship labels that you and your modelers can select from such as the sample set below.

- Contain

- Assign
- Categorize
- Group
- Classify
- Appear on
- Work for
- Own
- Manage
- Belong to

If a need for a new relationship label name comes up, have a simple process in place to have it added to your list.

Make sure indicators have a name that does not imply a choice.

For example, the indicator **Not For Sale Item Indicator** is confusing because if the value is Y for Yes, does that mean "Yes, the item is not for sale" or "No, the item is for sale." A better name would be **Item Sale Indicator**.

Make sure a surrogate key uses the entity as its prime followed the classword "ID" with the two separated by an underscore.

For example, **Employee_ID**. If your organization has a different naming structure for surrogate keys, it should be followed over this naming practice. Just make sure the policies are being followed consistently.

Make sure the physical names correspond to their logical names with approved abbreviations.

So for example, **Customer Last Name** becomes CUST_LAST_NM.

MODEL HAS CONSISTENT STYLE

Check that the model follows your organization's standard on style.

For example, if logical names should be initial uppercase with spaces, I would expect to see **Customer Account** instead of **CUSTOMER-ACCOUNT**. As an aside, upper case is more difficult to read and often brings emotion in for the reader as in an email containing uppercase text.

Summary of Standards Checks

Structure:
- ✓ Check that all entities are singular nouns.
- ✓ Check that all relationships are present tense verbs.
- ✓ Check that all attributes include a prime; zero, one, or more modifiers; and a classword.
- ✓ Catch relationship labels on a dimensional data model.
- ✓ Make sure the model does not exceed database-specific character limits.
- ✓ Make sure rolenames have the same prime and classword as their primary key.
- ✓ Check that attribute names are singular.
- ✓ Check that the name of each foreign key attribute matches the primary key unless role naming is being used.
- ✓ Ensure all attributes contain at most five modifiers.
- ✓ Make sure entity names do not end with a classword.
- ✓ Make sure the model avoids abbreviations and initialisms unless everyone knows what they mean.
- ✓ Catch any prepositions (e.g., at, by, for, from, in, of, to), articles (e.g., a, an, the), and conjunctions (e.g., and, or, but) used in any name.

Term:
- ✓ Check that a suffix of "Dimension" or "Fact" is used for all entities on a dimensional data model.
- ✓ Make sure each relationship label captures the business reason for the relationship.
- ✓ Make sure each relationship has a pre-approved relationship label.
- ✓ Make sure indicators have a name that does not imply a choice.
- ✓ Make sure a surrogate key uses the entity as its prime followed the classword "ID" with the two separated by an underscore.
- ✓ Make sure the physical names correspond to their logical names with approved abbreviations.

Style:
- ✓ Check that the model follows your organization's standard on style.

Chapter 10
Category Seven: Readability
How well has the model been arranged for readability?

The "Readability" category makes sure the model is visually easy to follow. This question is not the most important of the ten categories. However, if your model is difficult to read, you will not accurately address the more important categories on the scorecard. For example, if there are too many entities on a model printout, the model becomes hard to read and therefore also becomes less valuable as a communication tool.

To improve model readability, put yourself in your audiences' shoes. That is, if you were the person who needs to completely understand the model, how would you like to see it arranged to make it as easy to read as possible?

Leverage the readability features in your data modeling tool. ER/Studio for example, includes several default layout options as well as the ability to create submodels to make larger models easier to navigate. Readability needs to be considered at model, entity, attribute, and relationship levels.

CATEGORY EXPECTATIONS

This section contains a subset of what to look for to grade the Readability category.

MODEL IS READABLE

Make sure large complex models are broken into smaller pieces.

Knowing how and where to break up the data model into subject areas comes down to putting yourself in your reader's shoes and how they would like to view the model. For example, you may find that the **Order** entities are on one subject area (also known as a submodel) and relate to **Product,** which is also shown on the order subject area, but **Product** is modeled in much more detail in the **Product** subject area. So the **Product** entity in the **Order** subject area serves the role as a link to another subject area that elaborates on **Product** in much more detail. In each specific subject area, highlight the entities that are brought in or borrowed from other subject areas.

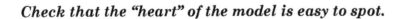

Check that the "heart" of the model is easy to spot.

That is, upon looking at a data model, which part of the model are your eyes naturally attracted toward? This tends to be an entity or entities with many relationships to other entities, similar to the hub on a bicycle tire with many spokes to the outside rim of the tire. This "heart" needs to be carefully positioned so that the reader can identify it early on and use this as a starting point to walk through the rest of the model.

Make sure the model does not contain more than two subtyping levels of subtyping.

When a data model contains more than two levels of subtyping, it starts losing readability. If there are more than two levels, many times this can be resolved by using multiple subtype trees. For example, on the data model below, we used three subtyping trees instead of having three levels of subtyping.

Before:

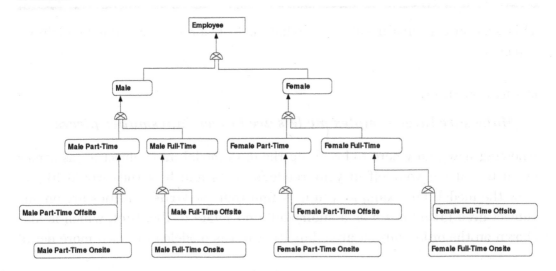

After:

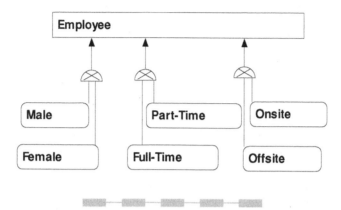

Recommend the Axis Technique for dimensional conceptual data models.

The Axis Technique is when you put the business process you are measuring in the center with each axis representing a dimension.

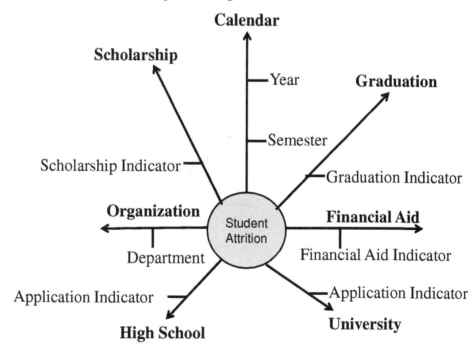

The notches on each axis represent the levels of detail that are required to see the measures in the meter. This form works very well when the audience has limited exposure to data modeling (or doesn't want to see the traditional data modeling symbols such as the crow's foot representing "many"). On the following model, **Student Attrition** is the business process shown in the center of the circle, and all of the different levels of detail we can view **Student Attrition** by are shown on the various axes.

ENTITY LAYOUT ACCEPTABLE

Ensure in dimensional data modeling that the meter goes in the center of the model surrounded by the dimensions, in either the standard or peacock layouts.

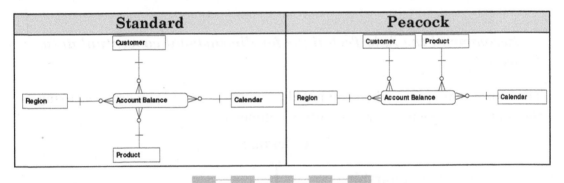

Ensure the modeler used alignment toolbars to evenly align entities.

Good data modeling tools like ER/Studio make it so easy to align and space entities.

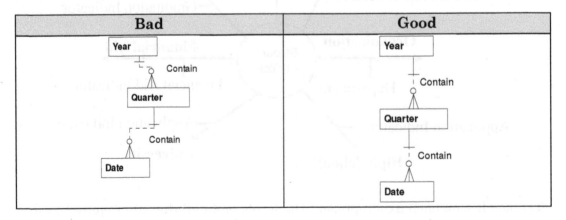

Ensure entities are easy to view against the background on a computer screen and also on a printout.

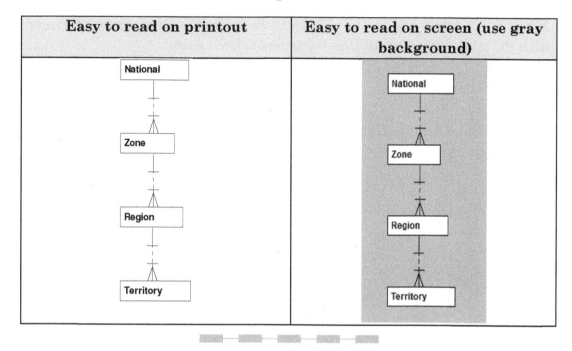

Check that font size on a data model is at least 8 pt font and ideally 11 pt font.

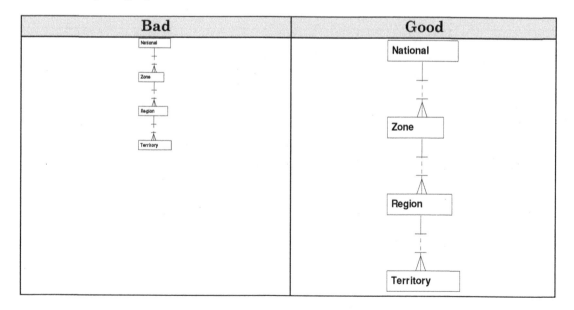

Check that the most important entities on a data model are emphasized.

Notice how **Order**, the meter and therefore most important entity, is larger than the other entities on the following dimensional model.

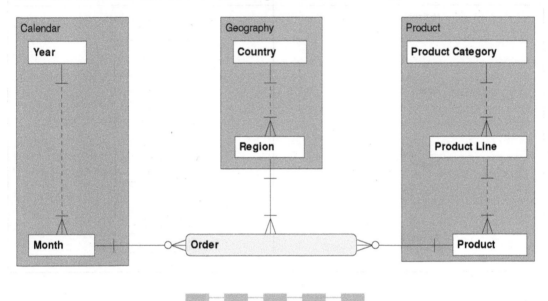

Make sure the parent entity goes above or parallel to the child entity.

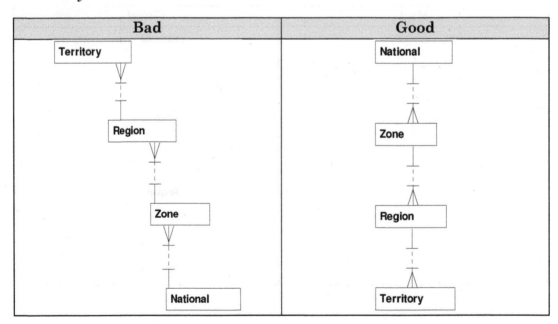

ATTRIBUTE SEQUENCE ACCEPTABLE

Ensure attributes in reference entities are listed in a sequence that makes sense to the business such as by chronology.

Attributes in reference entities (also known as master data or profile entities such as **Customer**, **Account**, and **Product**) should be listed in the order in which they appear to the business.

Bad	Good
Customer	**Customer**
Customer Number	Customer Number
Customer Last Name Customer Address Line Text Customer Country Code Customer State Code Customer Postal Code Customer First Name Customer City Name	Customer First Name Customer Last Name Customer Address Line Text Customer City Name Customer State Code Customer Postal Code Customer Country Code

Ensure attributes in transaction entities are grouped by classword.

Attributes in transaction entities (such as **Order**, **Credit**, and **Registration**) should be grouped by classword. I find with transaction entities containing a large amount of attributes that grouping them by classword makes it easier to find attributes.

Bad	Good
Sales Fact	**Sales Fact**
Calendar ID Product ID Customer ID	Calendar ID Product ID Customer ID
Sales Net Amount Sales Returned Quantity Sales Gross Amount Sales Total Quantity	Sales Net Amount Sales Gross Amount Sales Total Quantity Sales Returned Quantity

RELATIONSHIP LAYOUT ACCEPTABLE

Ensure the model minimizes relationship line length and the number of direction changes a relationship line makes.

It is much easier to read the relationships on a data model when the lines are as short and straight as possible. Direction changes in the relationship line can confuse the reader and make it difficult to see which entities are related. Note how straight the lines are in the following model.

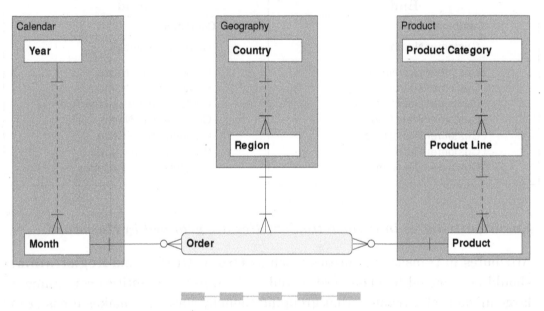

Ensure the model minimizes the number of crossings of relationship lines.

When too many entities are displayed on the same diagram, it can be hard to make out where relationship lines connect, and crossing the lines makes it harder. Reduce the number of crossings where possible, and if the diagram is still too busy, consider breaking it into more than one diagram.

Summary of Readability Checks

Model:
✓ Make sure large complex models are broken into smaller pieces.
✓ Check that the "heart" of the model is easy to spot.
✓ Make sure the model does not contain more than two levels of subtyping.
✓ Recommend the Axis Technique for dimensional conceptual data models.

Entity:
✓ Ensure in dimensional data modeling that the meter goes in the center of the model surrounded by the dimensions, in either the standard or peacock layouts.
✓ Ensure the modeler used alignment toolbars to evenly align entities.
✓ Ensure entities are easy to view against the background on a computer screen and also on a printout.
✓ Check that font size on a data model is at least 8 pt font and ideally 11 pt font.
✓ Check that the most important entities on a data model are emphasized.
✓ Make sure the parent entity goes above or parallel to the child entity.

Attribute:
✓ Ensure attributes in reference entities are listed in a sequence that makes sense to the business such as by chronology.
✓ Ensure attributes in transaction entities are grouped by classword.

Relationship:
✓ Ensure the model minimizes relationship line length and the number of direction changes a relationship line makes.
✓ Ensure the model minimizes the number of crossings of relationship lines.

The "Definitions" category reduces doubt about the meanings of the attributes and entities. Doubts and misinterpretations lead to model ambiguity. Good definitions support precision on the data model diagram. This category confirms all of the entity and attribute definitions have three characteristics: clarity, completeness, and correctness.

Clarity means that a reader can understand the meaning of a term by reading the definition only once. A clear definition does not require the reader to decipher how each sentence should be interpreted. The definition contains what the entity represents and not what the entity contains or where the entity is used.

Completeness means that the definition is at the appropriate level of detail and that it includes all of the necessary components such as derivations, synonyms, exceptions, and examples. Having a definition at the appropriate level of detail means that it is not so generic as to provide very little additional value nor so specific that it provides value only to an application or department—or so specific that it adds value only at a certain point in time.

Correctness means that the definition completely matches what the term means and is consistent with the rest of the business. An expert in the subject matter would agree that the term matches the definition.

For example, the following page contains a clear, complete, and correct definition for **Customer**. This is a clear definition because any ambiguous terms are clarified such as "normally" in the second sentence. The third sentence explains an example of a customer that does not purchase our products and therefore is outside the realm of being a "normal" purchase. Also, this definition is complete because it explains frequently confused terms with **Customer**, such as **Prospect** and **Consumer**, and examples of customers are provided. Examples are a very important part of the definition. This definition is correct assuming someone from the business (a credible source) signs off on this definition.

A Customer is a person or organization who obtains our product for resale. The Customer normally obtains the product through purchase. An example of a customer who does not purchase our product is the Salvation Army, which receives the product for free as a charity organization. A person or organization must have obtained at least one product from us to be considered a Customer. That is, Prospects are not Customers. Also, once a Customer, always a Customer so even Customers that have not obtained anything in 50 years are still considered Customers. The Customer is different than the Consumer, who purchases the product for consumption as opposed to resale.

Examples:
Walmart
Bob's Grocery Store
Military Base 1332

CATEGORY EXPECTATIONS

This section contains a subset of what to look for to grade the Definitions category.

DEFINITIONS ARE CLEAR

Do you know what the term means after just one reading through the definition? A clear definition does not require the reader to decipher how each sentence should be interpreted. The definition contains what the entity represents and not what the entity contains or where the entity is used.

Ensure industry generic definitions are made specific for your organization where needed.

Sometimes definitions may be copied from industry websites or glossaries. While it is possible that these definitions are sufficient, I have found in a majority of situations that these types of definitions are often more of starter definitions and need to be customized for a particular organization. You will see an example of such a definition in our Case Study in Chapter 16.

Check that each definition does not describe only what the entity contains.

Catch definitions that only describe what the object contains, such as this definition for **Customer**: "Customer contains last name, first name, and address." We can tell what the entity contains by looking at its list of attributes. An entity definition should say what the instance represents, not just what data is recorded about each instance.

Check that definitions do not contain obscure technical terminology and abbreviations.

Only expect to see terminology and abbreviations that the audience for the model is familiar with.

Bad	Good
ROTA Amount	Return On Total Assets Amount

DEFINITIONS ARE COMPLETE

Completeness means that the definition is at the appropriate level of detail and that it includes all of the necessary components, such as derivations, synonyms, exceptions, and examples.

Ensure identifier definitions are complete.

In definitions for identifiers, include in the definition additional information such as the scope of uniqueness (e.g., whether the identifier is unique within an application, within a department, within an organization, within an industry, etc.), the party responsible for assigning and managing the identifier, the structure (counter or one that contains business intelligence), business purpose, and whether the identifier can ever be reused or changed.

Check that examples are included with definitions of code attributes.

Without examples	With examples
The Gender Code is a short unique identifier for the gender name.	The Gender Code is a short unique identifier for the gender name. Examples: 01 = Male, 02 = Female

Ensure definitions for derived attributes contain derivations.

It is a good practice to describe how calculated attributes are calculated. For example, if **Gross Sales Amount** is calculated by multiplying **List Price** and **Order Quantity**, I would expect to see this calculation in the attribute's definition.

Check that there are no tautologies.

A tautology is a definition that is redundant with the name of the entity or attribute.

Bad	Good
Customer Identifier: The identifier for the customer.	Customer Identifier: The mandatory, unique, and stable element for recognizing a single customer. That is, if there are 100 customers, there will be 100 distinct Customer Identifier values. This identifier is unique within the Customer Relationship Management application and only within the North American market (not globally).

DEFINITIONS ARE CORRECT

Correctness means that the definition completely matches what the term means and is consistent with the rest of the business.

Check that definitions are consistent with other information we know about the attribute.

For example, **Customer Shoe Size** being defined as "The middle name of the customer" is something we need to catch. After raising this concern, if a business person says that this is the correct definition for **Customer Shoe Size**, we must accept it as the correct definition.

Check that definitions have been approved by a credible source.

Having someone from the data governance area, such as a credible business expert, validate the definition not only ensures we have the correct definition but also adds a lot of credibility to the data model.

Attributes from external sources should be referenced back to a specific version of the source documents.

For example, if **Customer Language Code** is the international standard on language codes, in the definition for this attribute we should reference the specification ISO639-3.

Summary of Definition Checks

Clear:
- ✓ Ensure industry generic definitions are made specific for your organization where needed.
- ✓ Check that each definition does not describe only what the entity contains.
- ✓ Check that definitions do not contain obscure technical terminology and abbreviations.

Complete:
- ✓ Ensure identifier definitions are complete.
- ✓ Check that examples are included with definitions of code attributes.
- ✓ Ensure definitions for derived attributes contain derivations.
- ✓ Check that there are no tautologies.

Correct:
- ✓ Check that definitions are consistent with other information we know about the attribute.
- ✓ Check that definitions have been approved by a credible source.
- ✓ Attributes from external sources should be referenced back to a specific version of the source documents.

Chapter 12
Category Nine: Consistency
How consistent is the model with the enterprise?

The "Consistency" category makes sure the data model complements the "big picture," usually in the form of an enterprise data model. The structures that appear in a data model should be consistent in terminology and usage with structures that appear in an enterprise data model, if one exists.

An enterprise data model (EDM) is a subject-oriented and integrated data model representing all of the data produced and consumed across an entire organization. Subject-oriented means that the concepts on a data model fit together as the CEO sees the company as opposed to how individual functional or department heads see their view of the company. Integration means that all of the data and rules in an organization are depicted once and fit together seamlessly.

For example, we need to catch when the data model being reviewed has an entity called **Customer**, yet on the enterprise data model the same concept is called **Consumer**.

Not all organizations have an enterprise data model. In the absence of an enterprise model, I look for widely accepted existing models for comparison such as the data models to support vendor applications (if they are accessible and intelligible) or industry models, which are models that are built for a particular industry or function.

If your organization does not have an enterprise data model or other accepted data model for comparison, or if the model you're reviewing **is** the EDM, you can remove this category and allocate the points for this category to the other nine categories.

CATEGORY EXPECTATIONS

This section contains a subset of what to look for to grade the Consistency category.

Check that entity names are consistent.

With names, be aware of the possibility of both synonyms and homonyms. Synonyms are when there are two or more names for the same term such as "Project XYZ calls it **Client**, but the enterprise calls it **Customer**." Homonyms are words with the same name but have different meanings. Homonyms can be very difficult to detect as sometimes differences can be very subtle. Knowing the states a concept goes through can help detect and correct these situations. For example, a marketing department might use the term **Customer** to refer to prospects, whereas the enterprise data model might only consider organizations that have already made a purchase to be considered a customer. Both marketing and the enterprise call it **Customer**, but it means two different things.

Bad	Good
An entity on the project data model is named **Customer**, yet on the enterprise data model the same concept is called **Consumer**.	An entity on the project data model is named **Customer**, and on the enterprise data model **Customer** is listed as a subtype of **Party Role**.

Check that entity definitions are consistent.

For example, if the definition for **Customer** on the model we are reviewing contradicts the definition for **Customer** on the enterprise data model, we need to catch this.

Check that attribute names are consistent.

For example, if the project data model has an attribute named "Customer Last Name" yet the enterprise data model calls this same attribute "Customer Surname," we need to catch this.

Check that attribute definitions are consistent.

For example, we need to catch if the definition for **Gross Sales Amount** on the data model we are reviewing has a different definition than **Gross Sales Amount** on the enterprise data model.

Check that attribute formatting is consistent.

For example, we need to catch if the length of **Customer Last Name** is 25 characters on the data model we are reviewing yet 50 characters on the enterprise data model.

Summary of Consistency Checks

✓ Check that entity names are consistent.

✓ Check that entity definitions are consistent.

✓ Check that attribute names are consistent.

✓ Check that attribute definitions are consistent.

✓ Check that attribute formatting is consistent.

The "Data" category determines how well the attributes and their rules match reality. Does the attribute **Customer Last Name** really contain the customer's last name, for example? This Data category is designed to reduce surprises and help ensure the structures on the model match the data these structures will be holding.

CATEGORY EXPECTATIONS

This section contains a subset of what to look for to grade the Data category.

Check for evidence that data profiling has been done.

On a logical or physical data model, I try to find out whether the modeler has seen the actual data that will eventually be loaded into the database. Often simple queries can be run against the attributes to profile the data. Examples include the minimum and maximum length of the data values, what percent of the time the attribute is null, results of foreign key to primary key joins, and average values of measures.

Ensure domains have been leveraged.

As mentioned earlier, a domain is a restricted set of values that can be assigned to an attribute. Domains increase application consistency, improve data quality, and reduce modeling time. Domains can be defined as a format, range, or list. For example, if a requirement requests knowing the employee's gender, we would expect to see a **Gender** list domain with values 01 for Male and 02 for Female.

Ensure code entities have been leveraged.

Look for opportunities where the application can benefit from code entities (also known as "reference entities"), which enforce valid values. Recently I was reviewing a data model for a manufacturing company that sells its products through an online catalog, and the key entity in this model was **Product**. **Product** contains all of the attributes required to describe the product in the company's catalog including weight and color. The color attribute was free form text, allowing the user to enter any possible color. However, there were only a fixed set of possible colors, and even with color variations there were less than 100 options. Therefore, I recommended that a color entity be created with a foreign key back to product.

Bad	Good
Product Product Code Product Name Product Description Text Product Color Name	**Product Color** Product Color Code Product Color Name ┆ Describe **Product** Product Code Product Color Code (FK) Product Name Product Description Text

There are several advantages of having a code entity instead of free form text using this color attribute as an example:

- **Easily handle names changes**. If the color names ever change (e.g. Orange-Red to Red-Orange) we make the change to the text once instead of for every occurrence it appears.

- **Increase data quality**. We can dramatically reduce spelling errors by storing the description only one time. Using 05 for the color Purple reduces the chance for spelling errors.

- **Allow for future expansion**. If in the future we decide that we would like to store the different language names for each color, having a separate entity for colors allows us to easily connect to another separate entity **Language**.

- **Populate a pick list of available values for data entry**. If specific values are in-use in existing data but not available for ongoing use, the code entity is a great place to record this availability.

- **Provide additional descriptive or help data for each selection**.

Ensure required attributes do not contain any null values.

Look for attributes defined as NOT NULL (required) or those which should be NOT NULL but where this has not been enforced yet and contain missing values in their data. This situation is most serious when the required attribute is a primary or alternate key.

Ensure attribute names are consistent with the data.

These are situations when the data is obviously completely different than what is implied by the attribute's name and definition. For example, **Customer Eye Color Text** contains the customer's shoe size. I remember working on a project where I was modeling a consumer feedback interface and a field that appeared in the interface was called **Company**. I assumed this was **Company Name** and modeled it as such, only to find out during testing that the **Company** field is where data entry people were populating the email addresses! I wish I knew this sooner as during testing it was too late to update the attribute name, so I was left with an attribute called "Company" that contained the email address.

Ensure each foreign key links back to its corresponding primary key.

We need to make sure the relationships on the data model match the actual data. We do this by checking that each foreign key value exists as its corresponding primary key value. We also check the cardinality. For example, if the foreign key value is NOT NULL, we need to make sure there is a value for every entity instance.

Ensure each attribute's format is consistent with its data.

For example, if we catch a five character year such as 99999 when the format is only four characters.

Summary of Data Checks

✓ Check for evidence that data profiling has been done.

✓ Ensure domains have been leveraged.

✓ Ensure code entities have been leveraged.

✓ Ensure required attributes do not contain any null values.

✓ Ensure attribute names are consistent with the data.

✓ Ensure each foreign key links back to its corresponding primary key.

✓ Ensure each attribute's format is consistent with its data.

In this section we will help you prepare for the model review (Chapter 14), provide tips for you to apply during the model review (Chapter 15) and then review a data model based upon one of my actual projects (Chapter 16).

Chapter 14
Preparing for the Model Review

This chapter helps you prepare for a successful model review. We will discuss both required and extra credit documentation, review structure, model chunks, seating pattern, and group participation.

REQUIRED DOCUMENTATION

The following checklist represents the required documentation for the review:

- **Data models to be reviewed**. Obvious but worth mentioning!

- **Entity and attribute definitions**. If we are provided with a data model file, often the definitions are included in this file. For example, double clicking on an entity brings up the entity definition. If we are not provided with a data model file, often the definitions will be provided in a separate document such as in a Microsoft Word file.

- **Supporting data models**. For example, if we are reviewing a logical data model, I would need to see the conceptual. If we are reviewing a physical data model, I would need to see both the conceptual and logical. If we are reviewing a dimensional, I would like to see the relational counterpart.

- **Requirements artifacts**. I need to see all of the requirements documents that were used to build the data model. This include formal requirements documents as well as interview write-ups, user stories, prototypes, data flow diagrams—anything that contributed to the development of the data model.

- **Naming standards**. The organization's naming standards practices including a list of abbreviations are required to review Category 6 of the Scorecard, the Standards category.

- **Enterprise data model**. The organization's current enterprise data model is required to review Category 9 of the Scorecard, the Consistency category. This model can be at the conceptual or logical level. If this model does not exist, we can remove the Consistency category as mentioned in Chapter 12.

- **Data profiling**. For Category 10, the Data category, we will need to see evidence that some level of data profiling was done if our data model being reviewed is a logical or physical data model.

EXTRA CREDIT DOCUMENTATION

The following checklist represents the extra credit documentation for the review:

- **Upstream and downstream data models and related lineage documentation**. This includes data models whose data will be loaded into the database based upon our model (upstream models), as well as data models whose database will receive data from our model (downstream models). These models are useful because we can confirm relationships, lengths, nullability, definitions, etc. If an attribute is defined as character(5) on our data model but that same attribute is character(10) on the upstream data model, we uncovered a correctness issue.

- **Customer-facing documents**. These are documents that are built to be seen by the customers of the project we are working on. "Customers" in this context typically includes external people or organizations who will purchase or use the products or services of the organization whose model we are reviewing. For example, once I reviewed a data model for a manufacturing company that sells most of its products through a catalog, and I made sure I had their latest catalog in front of me during the review. I was able to ask questions like "On page 25 of this catalog, for this particular product, where is the color of the product stored?"

Customers can also be internal such as a data model for an application that tracks employee satisfaction might have the human resources department as a customer.

- **Current stage of development**. This tells me how seriously my comments on the model will be taken. If an application for the data model I am reviewing is one week from going into production (this happened to me), I am pretty certain any comments I make will not be adopted. Likewise, if an application is still in its early stages of development, comments we provide can be addressed on the model and have a very positive impact.

- **Issues list**. Most modeling projects include a list of outstanding issues.

- **Additional rules list**. An example of a rule that would appear in this additional document would be "Freshman students can register for at most 18 credits a semester." This rule cannot be captured on an entity-relationship diagram and so should appear in this extra document.

REVIEW STRUCTURE

It is better to have four two-hour model reviews than one eight-hour model review. Modeling is one of those activities that at times require simply working on something else for a while and then coming back to the review. I have had modeling revelations a few minutes after picking up a model, whereas a day earlier it seemed impossible to come up with a creative solution.

DIVIDE THE MODEL UP INTO REALISTIC CHUNKS FOR REVIEW

The modeler needs to decide the best approach to walk through the model, including how to break the model down into manageable chunks, where each chunk can be completed in a single meeting. If the data model is relatively small, it can be reviewed in a single meeting. If the data model is large, such as the following model, the data modeler needs to decide the best way to break it up into review pieces.

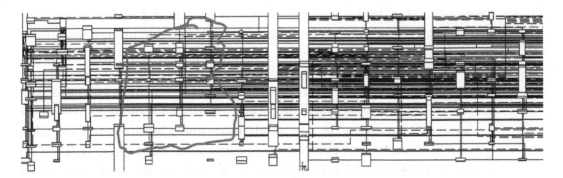

The modeler has already begun to chunk this model into review pieces, as can be seen with the outline made around a subset of the entities. Once the review of this model subset is complete, the next review meeting can start off discussing the changes made to this subset based on the prior meeting, and then the next subset can be discussed.

DECIDING WHO PARTICIPATES IN THE REVIEW

If the data model being reviewed is a conceptual, at a minimum we will need business analysts as part of the review. If the model is a logical, we would need at a minimum data modelers or data architects as part of the review. If the model is a physical, we will need at a minimum database administrators or developers to be involved.

If you work on a team of data modelers, you may find there is a review within the data modeling team at the end of each modeling phase before the next model is started. That is, before the logical data modeling can start, the conceptual data model must be reviewed and approved by the data modeling group. Before the physical data modeling can start, the logical data model must be reviewed and approved by the data modeling group.

Because decisions about the model will have impacts on the implementation of any application code, consider having an experienced developer on the review panel to assist with estimating the cost impacts.

SEATING PATTERN

My favorite seating pattern for a model review is a round table with enough room around the table for everyone to be comfortable and have a copy of the data model in front of them. The reason I like the round table is that it promotes friendly conversation and no one person is in a seat that implies extra power or attention. Everyone is working together towards the single goal of a high quality data model.

Although it is probably the most common seating arrangement in most organizations, the boardroom table is not my favorite. I find that at least one participant winds up sitting in a seat which conveys power or attention. For example, at the head of the table, a reviewer might become more confrontational. If the person whose model we are reviewing sits at the head of the table, they might feel more self-conscious or defensive. If this is the type of table you have, consider not using the ends, just the sides. Often there will be a projection screen at one end anyway.

The lecture style might work effectively if a large part of the review is the modeler walking through the model. This way the model can be displayed on a screen and the modeler can zoom in and out as the different structures of the model are discussed.

Chapter 15
During the Model Review

This chapter provides tips for you to apply during the model review.

CHOOSE A MILE DEEP OVER A MILE WIDE

As mentioned during the prior chapter, I am a believer in breaking the data model into manageable chunks for review. I would rather see four chunks of two-hour meetings instead of one long eight-hour meeting. This allows the review to be a "deep dive" as opposed to a "broad brush" approach. A "deep dive" means we are discussing the detailed content of the model, as opposed to a "broad brush" approach, which is usually too high level to produce valuable comments. Usually with a "broad brush" approach, comments are only mildly useful, such as:

- I found a crossing relationship line here.

- **Customer Last Name** should be 50 characters instead of 40.

- **Account Open Date** has a spelling error.

With a "deep dive" approach, however, the comments tend to be much richer and more valuable such as, "I see how you modeled **Order**, but I modeled **Order** slightly differently on a recent assignment. Let's compare the two models attribute by attribute to make sure we are consistent."

Often a review will find systematic errors during a deep dive that result in sending the whole model back for rework before reconvening. In this case, you can cut your review short. There's no need to record every instance of a systematic error as long as it is systematically fixed.

SET THE STAGE

It is critical that as much emotion as possible be filtered out of the Scorecard work. It is very easy to get attached to the model and translate areas for improvement on the model with weaknesses of the data modeler. We should not connect the model with the modeler when applying the Scorecard.

If you are one of the reviewers, realize that the modeler might be offended by certain comments. Similarly, if your model is being reviewed, take the negative comments on the model in perspective. Your data modeling skills are not being criticized; rather, everyone including you is looking to create a better data model so all comments, both positive and negative, need to be welcome.

I often like to start off a model review by talking about each of our roles during the review. I make a point of saying that the person who created the data model we are reviewing today is not playing the role of the data modeler who built the data model, but instead playing the role of the expert who knows more about this model than anybody else. This way the modeler will feel less like they are being attacked and more like the knowledgeable expert that they really are!

BUILD A SUPPORT GROUP

One of the challenges with reviewing the model with other modelers, however, is that in today's lean organizations, there aren't many people just doing modeling. Years ago, I worked in a group that had nine data modelers full time. Later, I worked on a team that had six data modelers full time. On my next assignment, though, I was the only full-time data modeler! In situations like this, it is best to borrow some time from a modeler on a related project or perhaps find out if your organization has a person who reviews models for best practice guidelines, at least part time.

At a large beverage company I'm familiar with, they review models by having a weekly model review forum, where they bring in pizza and soda, and anyone can bring in their models to be reviewed by the organization's senior data modelers. It is a great way to get input on your data model.

AVERAGE THE SCORES

Not everyone grades the same way; there are easy graders and strict graders. An easy grader may give four out of five, a strict grader two out of five. By reviewing models in groups or averaging scores, a more objective final score can be achieved such as three out of five.

START WITH A CDM

If you are reviewing a logical or physical data model, starting off with a CDM can be a great way to equalize everyone and not scare anyone away with a large complex data model. First walk through the conceptual, and then start the review of the detailed model subset. For example, I once had to walk through an extremely complex module in SAP, so I started off with a conceptual data model first to give everyone the big picture.

KNOW WHEN TO THROW IN THE TOWEL

Try to avoid going beyond a two-hour review, but stop even sooner if you feel fatigue is facing the group. I have been in very passionate model reviews, and I think some of the reasons for people yelling, banging their shoe on the table, or crying, had to do with content overload and repetition. If we can detect that situations like these are brewing, we can react sooner and reschedule the review to a time when everyone is feeling refreshed.

KEEP IT FUN

You can make model reviews something all of the reviewers look forward to. Keep the atmosphere light, and maybe bring in goodies for reviewers such as snacks and beverages.

For this case study, we will review the data model underlying an application that will support trends on consumer feedback. This application, called *Consumer Interaction*, analyzes three types of consumer interactions: complaints, compliments and questions. An interaction is a contact between an employee and a consumer for a specific product. An interaction can take place through a variety of medium such as through phone, email, and mail.

Here are examples of some of the interactions:

- "I love your product." (compliment)

- "I hate your product." (complaint)

- "I found a strange object in your product." (complaint)

- "Where can I buy your product?" (question)

- "I found your product difficult to assemble." (complaint)

A consumer can have many interactions on many products. For example, Bob can call Monday because he did not like Product XYZ, he can call Tuesday and say that he now likes Product XYZ, and can call Wednesday and say that he loves Product ABC. Consumer Interaction in this example would contain three records, and at a high level look something like this:

Consumer	Product	Employee	Interaction	Date received
Bob	XYZ	Mary	I don't like this product.	Monday 4/1/2015
Bob	XYZ	Jane	I love this product!	Tuesday 4/2/2015
Bob	ABC	Mary	This product is pretty good.	Wednesday 4/3/2015

The requirement is to produce a report for each product that shows for the previous 12 months the number of complaints, compliments and questions. This report has to allow the users to "drill down" to get to the interaction level of detail and see the actual interaction such as "Loved product." See bar chart below.

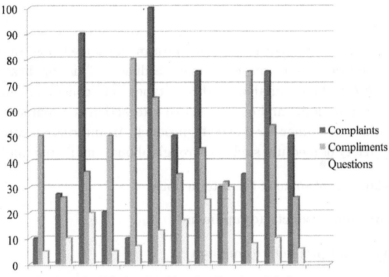

Here is the data model we are going to review:

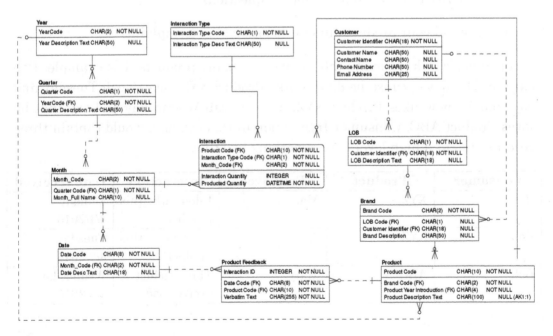

There is a calendar hierarchy, where **Year** is broken down into **Quarters**, then into **Months**, and finally into the lowest level **Date**. There also appears to be a product hierarchy, where a **Product** rolls up to a **Brand**, which rolls up to a **LOB** (Line of Business, similar to a subsidiary), which rolls up to a **Customer**. We learn that **Customer** is not the person who calls up with an interaction but is instead the organization whose product the interaction is about. So for example, the **Customer** could be `Mercedes Benz`, the **LOB** the model such as the `S-Class`, the **Brand** the trim package such as the `Maybach S600 Sedan`, and the **Product** the specific auto. The **Product Code** could be a **Vehicle Identification Number**.

Interaction Type contains only three values:

Interaction Type Code	Interaction Type Desc Text
01	Complaint
02	Compliment
03	Question

Interaction captures the bar chart. **Interaction Quantity** contains the number of people that complained, complimented, or questioned a particular product in a particular month. **Produced Quantity** (which contains a spelling error on the model which will be caught in the naming standards category) wasn't specifically part of the requirements, but the modeler felt it would be important to know how many of a product was produced to gauge the significance of the feedback. For example, if five complaints were received and only five were produced, it tells us something very different than if five complaints were received but five million were produced.

Product Feedback contains the actual interaction in the attribute **Verbatim Text** such as "`Found something strange in the product.`"

Let's now review this model for all ten categories.

1. CORRECTNESS

There are two requirements our model must satisfy: 1) produce the bar chart and 2) allow the end-users to drill down to the interaction level of detail.

The entity **Interaction** contains the **Interaction Quantity** for a particular **Product**, **Interaction Type**, and **Month**, which is needed to produce the bar chart. So the first requirement is satisfied on the model. If there were 50 complaints for product XYZ in June, **Interaction Quantity** would contain the value 50, **Product Code** would reference back to product XYZ, **Interaction Type Code** would contain a 01 for a complaint, and **Month_Code** would contain 06 for June.

We now need to get to the interaction level of detail and see the actual interaction. If, for example, someone double clicks on the bar that says that 50 complaints were received for a particular product in a given month, we would expect what will appear are all 50 complaints along with the date each complaint occurred. **Product Feedback** appears to be the entity storing the detailed feedback from the consumer within the attribute **Verbatim Text**.

Following the relationships from **Interaction** to **Month** to **Date** to **Product Feedback**, we see we can navigate from 50 interactions in April down to the detailed dates of each interaction. In addition, there are relationships to **Product** from **Interaction** and **Product Feedback**, allowing us to identify the product at the lowest level as well. However, we see that there is a crucial relationship missing—the one from **Interaction Type** down to **Product Feedback**. We cannot identify on the **Product Feedback** entity whether the interaction is a complaint, compliment, or question. We can capture that 50 interactions for Product XYZ took place during April, but we do not know whether these comments were complaints, compliments, or questions. This means we cannot satisfy the second requirement on the model.

Therefore the highest number of points we can give this model for Correctness will be half because we can satisfy only half the requirements—just the first requirement and not the second. Therefore we will give seven out of 15 points for this category.

Once we add the missing relationship from **Interaction Type** down to **Product Feedback**, this model will get a perfect score on Correctness.

2. COMPLETENESS

Completeness means we have all of the necessary information for each requirement, and also that we have all of the metadata.

In terms of completeness of requirements, we look for parts of requirements that were asked for but we cannot find on the model as well as the other way around—structures that were added to the model but not requested in a requirement. On this model we find both of these situations.

The only requirement given in terms of calendar was to be able to see complaints, compliments, and questions at a month level and then drill down to a date level. However, the model also contains the higher levels of **Year** and **Quarter**. We will need to highlight **Year** and **Quarter** and mark them as out-of-scope and therefore as a completeness issue. You might be thinking that it may make sense to keep **Year** and **Quarter** just in case the requirements change or expand so we need to see complaints at a **Year** and **Quarter** level too. However, if it was not part of a requirement, we need to raise it to the business and have them decide whether it should be added as a requirement, and then possibly the scope of the project will expand. It is always easy to add a few structures to the data model, yet it could be much more difficult to implement these extra structures. There is a cost to everything, and therefore we need to challenge those sections of the model not explicitly requested in requirements.

Applying the same logic to other parts of the model, do we really need to have **Customer, LOB,** and **Brand** on the model? The requirement was to see the number of **Complaints, Compliments,** and **Questions** for each **Product**. Nothing was mentioned though about the product hierarchy of **Brand, LOB,** and **Customer**. So these three additional levels should also be flagged as part of Completeness. Having **Customer** as the highest level in the **Product** hierarchy concerns me anyway, so raising this structure as being out of scope is a good idea.

We can also analyze the attributes with an eye for completeness. For example, even though **Produced Quantity** appears to be a useful measure for determining the significance of the number of complaints, compliments, and questions, it was not mentioned in the requirements. We should therefore highlight **Produced Quantity** in the completeness category and have a business professional or business analyst decide whether it should be added. Perhaps knowing the produced quantity is of limited value because if someone complains about a product, that product was probably produced in an earlier month than what this attribute stores anyway. For example, if someone complains about a candy bar in July 2015, storing how much was produced in July 2015 has limited value because that particular candy bar was probably produced at least several months earlier. Maybe **Sales Quantity** would be a more appropriate attribute. Raising the issue will lead to having a healthy conversation to determine what is really needed.

Is there anything in any requirement that does not appear on the model? That is, are we missing any parts of the requirements? We could be. There is a very ambiguous phrase that was given to us in the requirements: *This report has to allow the users to "drill down" to get to the interaction level of detail and see the actual interaction such as "Loved product".*

What is meant by "interaction level of detail"? I have seen phrases like this in many requirements documents. Phrases that refer to seeing the details are ambiguous because we do not know what the *details* are. For this project, do the details include knowing the consumer who placed the interaction or the employee who received the interaction? If yes, consumer and employee information need to appear on the model. We need to highlight this ambiguous phrase in the requirements document and make sure it gets elaborated as part of the completeness category.

I would give a very low score for completeness for this model. In fact, I probably would say something like "Instead of us continuing this review and scoring the model, let's meet again on Tuesday after the model has been updated with our feedback and we will review the model again for all ten categories." This way we do not need to give a score to this model, and in the next round we may catch new items that need to be addressed. If we did score the completeness category for this model, three points out of 15 would be generous.

3. SCHEME

Scheme means that the model we are reviewing matches our expectation for its level of detail (conceptual, logical, and physical) and whether it is relational, dimensional, or NoSQL.

We need to ask the modeler what scheme this is. If there is a moment's hesitation on the part of the modeler to answer this question, the "danger, danger" alarm should go off in our head as it may not be clear to the modeler the model scheme of their own model.

In the absence of someone to question, we will need to play detective and see if we can determine the scheme. Sometimes it is very easy, and in these cases often the scheme category receives a high score. Sometimes it is not so easy, as in this model's case, and the scoring will reflect this.

For example, we can rule out conceptual as the level of detail for this model because there are attributes on the model. So is this model a logical or physical? It definitely has some properties of a physical data model: database-specific formatting like CHAR(100) and DATETIME are giveaways this model could be a physical. So is showing whether an attribute is NULL or not (optional or mandatory). However, there is even more evidence that the model is logical; many of the attribute names are fully spelled out with spaces in between the terms.

Is this model relational or dimensional? **Product Feedback** is a relational component because it is storing the actual interaction in the attribute **Verbatim Text**, which is not a measure and therefore **Product Feedback** is not a meter. So the structure consisting of **Product Feedback** and its relationships to **Date** and **Product** are relational and not dimensional. Perhaps some automated sentiment analyzer might use this field to produce a numerical measure that approximates how positive or negative the feedback was, but the feedback itself is not a measure. However, the rest of the model appears to be dimensional. We have calendar, product, and interaction type dimensions, and **Interaction** is the meter which determines the health of the interaction process.

If we had to choose one cell to assign this model to, based on the above discussion, we would assign it to the dimensional logical cell and grade it there as such.

In additional to catching the relational component **Product Feedback**, this model has several other dimensional model violations. We would not expect to see zeros on the relationships between dimensional levels. That is, there can be no empty nodes in a dimensional hierarchy. For example, a **Customer** must have a **LOB**, yet on the model this appears as optional. It is acceptable to even make up values (such as 99) to ensure each node in a dimensional hierarchy has a value. So we would need to remove the zeros between **Customer** and **LOB**, **LOB** and **Brand**, **Brand** and **Product**, **Year** and **Month**, **Quarter** and **Month**, and **Month** and **Date**. Also, it is not a best practice to have relationships across dimensions, so we would need to catch the relationship from **Year** to **Product**. In the spirit of keeping the dimensional model simple, that relationship line from **Customer** to **Brand** should also be caught and most likely will go away once we make the hierarchies mandatory.

Due to all of these violations, this model would get a very low score in the Scheme category. If this was an actual model review, I would stop the review at this point and recommend changes be made and then the model be reviewed again from the beginning. This way, we do not have to give such a low score as the model would receive at most a three out of ten in this category in the model's present state.

4. STRUCTURE

"Structure" means we validate the design practices employed to build the model. There are three categories of structural soundness issues: *Consistency*, *Integrity*, and *Core*. Consistency means that if there are two or more of the same attribute on the data model, everything about these duplicated attributes matches such as formatting, lengths, and definitions. Integrity means a database structure can be generated from the data model. Core means that the basic rules of data modeling are being followed.

In terms of consistency, we see that **YearCode** from **Year** is two characters, yet as a foreign key in **Product**, **Product Year Introduction** is four characters. This is an example of a format mismatch between primary and foreign key. We also note that **Produced Quantity** has a datetime format when we would expect a quantity format. This is an example of a classword / format mismatch.

The calendar structure has some integrity issues. The primary key to **Quarter** is **Quarter Code**, which is a one character field. I would assume (and have to confirm) the values are 1, 2, 3, and 4. Yet **Quarter** contains a foreign key back to **Year**. So there is no way without changing the primary key structure to represent both `Quarter 1 2015` and `Quarter 1 2014`. Similarly with the **Month** structure, having a two character **Month Code** primary key means we can represent `December` as `12` but cannot capture `December 2015` and `December 2014`.

Product Description Text is a NULL alternate key in Product. NULL candidate keys are also integrity issues we need to raise.

The only core issue we may raise is that most of the entities have all null non-primary key attributes. For example, in **Customer** all of the attributes with the exception of **Customer Identifier** are null, allowing a customer to be identified but not described.

There are quite a few structural soundness issues on our model; therefore, I would recommend the modeler making these changes before the model is scored, or giving a very low score like three out of 15.

5. ABSTRACTION

To receive a high score on the abstraction category, a model will need to have the right balance between flexibility and simplicity. On this model, the only abstract entity is **Interaction Type**, which contains three values: a `1` for `Compliment`, a `2` for `Complaint`, and a `3` for `Question`. A dimensional data model is built for Simplicity, Speed, and Security. Abstraction is neither simple nor speedy, so therefore we would expect to see little if any abstraction on a dimensional data model.

However, we know why **Interaction Type** appears on the model as once the missing relationship from **Interaction Type** to **Product Feedback** is created, we can navigate from **Interaction** to **Product Feedback** to get to the interaction level of detail.

So of all ten categories we are reviewing, if the model is to get a perfect score in any category, it would be abstraction. This model has the right balance of abstraction—just enough to allow for navigation and no more. A perfect ten points in the abstraction category!

6. STANDARDS

"Standards" means we ensure the data model adheres to naming structure, term, and style.

This data model has fairly good structure. All of the entities are singular nouns and most of the attribute names contain the three main sections of prime, modifier, and classword. Some of the primes are missing such as in **Email Address**, **Phone Number**, and **Verbatim Text**. Whose email address and phone number is this, and what is the verbatim text describing? The prime would help here. Also is the proper classword "description" or "text"? Both are used inconsistently in this model.

Term also is fairly consistent on the model. Exceptions include **Customer;** unless the business uses this term consistently to represent the manufacturer, a better name would be **Manufacturer**. Also, the term "description" is sometimes abbreviated as "Desc" and sometimes fully spelled out as "Description." There is a spelling error in the attribute **Produced Quantity** (Producted instead of Produced); we will raise spelling errors as well as part of term. Also, unless everyone knows what **LOB** stands for, I would recommend spelling out **Line of Business**.

Style has a high amount of inconsistency in the model. Sometimes underscores are used to separate terms, sometimes spaces, sometimes camel case, and sometimes a combination of different styles such as **Month_Full Name**.

Due to a fair amount of consistency in applying naming standards, I would give this model a three out of five.

7. READABILITY

Readability means we make sure the model is visually easy to follow. Although, this model is arranged in a general dimensional modeling structure with the meter in the model surrounded by the dimensions, there are quite a few changes we can make to the model to make it easier to read.

Good data modeling tools like ER/Studio have auto-align and left and right justify buttons that can easily align the dimensions properly and space them evenly. We should also move the dimensions out more so they are more easily to distinguish as separate dimensions.

Get rid of lightning bolts (crooked relationship lines), such as the relationship line between **Interaction Type** and **Interaction** and between **Quarter** and **Month**.

The relationship line between **Interaction** and **Product** goes up and around the product dimension, making it very difficult to follow. It would be a lot easier to read if it went directly from **Interaction** to **Product**. Also, the relationship line from **Year** to **Product** can be made more readable by moving **Product** down slightly to remove one relationship bend, and moving **Year** out slightly will remove another relationship bend. The relationship line between **Customer** and **Brand** also can be aligned to make it easier to read.

Overall, because the model does resemble the traditional dimensional data model structure, I would rate this model a three out of five.

8. DEFINITIONS

Definitions mean we ensure no doubt exists about the contents of attributes and the relationships between entities. This category confirms all definitions have three characteristics: clarity, completeness, and correctness.

The following table contains all of the definitions we were provided with on this model:

Table Name	Column Name	Column Comment
Product Feedback	Interaction ID	
	Verbatim Text	The actual comment from the consumer who contacted us, such as "I found something in my product."
	Date Code	The full date in YYYYMMDD format.
	Product Code	The unique way of identifying the product. This is a business natural key.
Date	Date Code	The full date in YYYYMMDD format.
	Date Desc Text	
	Month_Code	The code for the month, a number between 01 and 12.
Interaction Type	Interaction Type Code	The code corresponding to whether the interaction with the consumer is a complaint, compliment, or question. Examples: 01 = Complaint 02 = Compliment 03 = Question
	Interaction Type Desc Text	The description corresponding to whether the interaction with the consumer is a complaint, compliment, or question. Examples: 01 = Complaint 02 = Compliment 03 = Question
Interaction	Interaction Quantity	The number of interactions.
	Producted Quantity	The amount of product produced.
	Product Code	The unique way of identifying the product. This is a business natural key.

Table Name	Column Name	Column Comment
	Interaction Type Code	The code corresponding to whether the interaction with the consumer is a complaint, compliment, or question. Examples: 01 = Complaint 02 = Compliment 03 = Question
	Month_Code	The code for the month, a number between 01 and 12.
Month	Month_Code	The code for the month, a number between 01 and 12.
	Month_Full Name	The name for the month.
	Quarter Code	The number 1, 2, 3, or 4 depending on which fourth of the year it is.
Year	YearCode	The four digit code (e.g. 2015) for the period of 365 days (or 366 days in leap years) starting from the first of January, used for reckoning time in ordinary affairs.
	Year Description Text	The text description for the period of 365 days (or 366 days in leap years) starting from the first of January, used for reckoning time in ordinary affairs.
Quarter	Quarter Code	The number 1, 2, 3, or 4 depending on which fourth of the year it is.
	Quarter Description Text	The full description for the quarter of year.
	YearCode	The four digit code (e.g. 2015) for the period of 365 days (or 366 days in leap years) starting from the first of January, used for reckoning time in ordinary affairs.
Customer	Customer Identifier	The identifier for the customer.
	Customer Name	Customer Name.

Table Name	Column Name	Column Comment
	Contact Name	The first and last name of the key person to reach at the Customer site. This is usually someone in Consumer Affairs.
	Phone Number	Contact phone number.
	Email Address	Contact email address.
LOB	LOB Code	The 2 character code corresponding to the line of business. Examples: 01 = Automobiles 02 = Motocycles 03 = Trucks
	LOB Description Text	The description corresponding to the line of business. Examples: 01 = Automobiles 02 = Motocycles 03 = Trucks
	Customer Identifier	The identifier for the customer.
Brand	Brand Code	The American Marketing Association defines a brand as a "name, term, design, symbol, or any other feature that identifies one seller's good or service as distinct from those of other sellers. The legal term for brand is trademark. A brand may identify one item, a family of items, or all items of that seller. If used for the firm as a whole, the preferred term is trade name."
	Brand Description	
	LOB Code	The 2 character code corresponding to the line of business. Examples: 01 = Automobiles 02 = Motocycles 03 = Trucks

Table Name	Column Name	Column Comment
	Customer Identifier	The identifier for the customer.
Product	Product Code	The unique way of identifying the product. This is a business natural key.
	Product Description Text	
	Brand Code	The American Marketing Association defines a brand as a "name, term, design, symbol, or any other feature that identifies one seller's good or service as distinct from those of other sellers. The legal term for brand is trademark. A brand may identify one item, a family of items, or all items of that seller. If used for the firm as a whole, the preferred term is trade name."
	Product Year Introduction	The four digit code (e.g. 2015) for the period of 365 days (or 366 days in leap years) starting from the first of January, used for reckoning time in ordinary affairs.

What score from zero to ten would you give for the Definitions category based upon these definitions?

Right away we notice that the entity definitions are missing. Therefore I would subtract half the points, so the highest score we can give is now five instead of ten.

In addition, a number of the attribute definitions are missing. Some of these missing definitions are more severe than others. Missing a definition for a primary key such as **Interaction ID,** for example, is more significant than missing a definition for **Date Desc Text**, but all missing definitions are important flags to raise.

Some of these definitions define formatting instead of what the attribute is. For example, **Date Code's** definition of "The full date in YYYYMMDD format."

Some of these definitions are tautologies (attributes defined only using their names), such as **Customer Name** being defined by "Customer Name" and **Customer Identifier** defined as "The identifier for the customer."

Still other definitions raise questions, such as the definition of **Phone Number**: "Contact phone number." The term "contact," however, has not been discussed previously. Is "contact" a new entity that needs to be added to the model?

There are also spelling errors in some of these definitions, such as "Motocycles" instead of "Motorcycles" in the definitions for **LOB Code** and **LOB Description Text**.

What do you think about the definition for **Brand Code**? It appears that this definition was copied from an industry definition. This could be a good starter definition, but does this organization's definition of brand really match 100% this industry definition? Most likely this definition will need to be customized to make it useful. Also, this generic definition for brand might be more appropriate for the entity **Brand** instead of for the attribute **Brand Code**.

Showing examples for the code definitions such as for **LOB Code** are great ideas. In these definitions, though, the same codes and values were used as examples for both the **LOB Code** and **LOB Description Text**. It could be confusing to see the same exact examples for different attributes.

Based on the overall poor quality of these definitions, I would score this model with a three out of ten.

9. CONSISTENCY

Consistency means we make sure the data model complements the "big picture," usually in the form of an enterprise data model.

We were not provided with an enterprise data model for this review, and many of the real models I review are not accompanied with an enterprise data model. Either there is an enterprise data model that exists that we need to ask for, or no enterprise data model exists. If no enterprise data model exists, we can remove this category and allocate the five points to another category. We will allocate these points to the next category, data, in this case study.

10. DATA

Data means we determine how well the attributes and their rules match the actual data that will be stored in the resulting database. For this category, let's focus in on just two of the entities on our model:

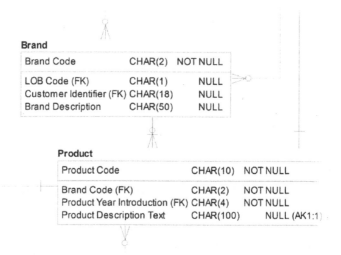

Below are a representative set of data for each of the entities on this model subset. Anything you would catch on the model in this category?

Brand

Brand Code	LOB Code	Cust ID	Brand Desc
W1	Q4	391238198	Widgets
	Q4	321912999	
W9		2919128920	Wizards
99			
B3	B2	392191	Warlords

Product

Product Code	Brand Code	Year Introduction	Product Desc
M43431	WI	11	Widget Light
B45328	W1		Widget Heavy
NA		99999	Not Applicable
C21392	B3	2010	Evil Warlords
47	W99	1999	Good Wizards

Here are a few flags to raise:

- **Brand Code** is the primary key of **Brand**, and therefore it is a required attribute. Yet the second record in **Brand** is missing its primary key.

- Anytime I see 99 or NA (for Not Applicable) as a value, I challenge it. Usually dummy values such as these are ways to get around the business rules, and we need to find out what those business rules are and the driver behind circumventing them.

- **LOB Code** is defined as one character in length, yet the actual values show two characters are needed instead.

- I would expect **Cust ID** to have the same length for each attribute such as nine characters as in the first two cases. So when I see an extra zero at the end or a shorter length such as 392191, I catch these.

- **Product Codes** of NA and 47 are eyebrow raisers as the other values are all six characters in length.

- There is a three-character **Brand Code**, W99. In addition W99 does not exist in the **Brand** entity. W9 exists, though, and it is possible after the last nine is truncated, everything may join just fine. But who wants that nine truncated? That is asking for trouble.

- There is a two-digit year and a five digit year.

Based upon all of these issues, this category would receive a low score, at most two.

COMPLETED SCORECARD

Here is a completed Scorecard for this model:

#	Category	Total score	Model score	%	Comments
1	How well does the model capture the requirements?	15	7		
2	How complete is the model?	15	3		
3	How well does the model match its scheme?	10	3		
4	How structurally sound is the model?	15	3		
5	How well does the model leverage generic structures?	10	10		
6	How well does the model follow naming standards?	5	3		
7	How well has the model been arranged for readability?	5	3		
8	How good are the definitions?	10	3		
9	How consistent is the model with the enterprise?	0	0		No enterprise data model, so these 5 points have been moved to Category 10.
10	How well does the metadata match the data?	15	2		
	TOTAL SCORE	100	37		

Obviously this data model did not pass. Usually, if the data model gets a very low score on one or more of the Correctness, Completeness, Scheme, and Structure categories, it is best to end the review and request the model be updated and then reviewed another time. This way we do not need to present such a low score, and there is a good chance when we review the model in the next go around, we will identify additional areas that need to be addressed.

Index

Bold page numbers indicate where terms are defined.